THEOLOGY OF THE LOVE OF GOD

George M. Newlands

John Knox Press
ATLANTA

Library of Congress Cataloging in Publication Data

Newlands, G M 1941-
　　Theology of the love of God.

　　Includes bibliographical references and index.
　　1. God—Love. 2. Love (Theology) I. Title.
BT140.N48 1981 231'.6 80-22547
ISBN 0-8042-0726-7

First published in Great Britain in 1980 by William Collins, Sons & Company, Ltd., London.

Copyright 1980 © George Newlands

A John Knox Press book published by arrangement with William Collins, Sons & Company, Ltd., London.

10 9 8 7 6 5 4 3 2 1

Printed in the United States of America

Atlanta, Georgia 30365

Contents

Introduction   9

1 Theology and the God who Loves   13
2 Love as Focus   26
3 Faith, Hope and Love in Christian Tradition   37
4 God's Love and Human Understanding   53
5 Towards a Critical Theology of Love   65
6 God's Love and the Basic Structures of Theology   80
7 The Love of God the Creator   95
8 The Love of God the Creator of Man   112
9 The Love of God the Reconciler   138
10 Love and the Nature of Salvation   155
11 God's Love in Christ, in Christian Thought   171
12 Love and the Understanding of Christ   185
13 The Love of God the Spirit in History   201

Index   217

For Elizabeth

Introduction

Talk of God is notoriously complex, and talk of love notoriously sentimental. But it seems to me that there is still a great deal to be quarried from the implications for theology of the central Christian affirmation that God is in his essential nature love, love characterized precisely and uniquely in the self-giving of God to mankind in the events surrounding the life, death and resurrection of Jesus Christ.

This is a study in systematic theology. My primary concern is with the material content of doctrine. But the Christian gospel is intended to be made available and comprehensible not only to people who are already members of the churches but to all men. We live in a world of men of many faiths or none, in which, indeed, Christians themselves work and think in a number of overlapping intellectual communities. It follows that the theologian, in carrying further the long process of development of the implications of the substantive content of faith, will naturally seek at every turn to relate his work to the questions which men ask about themselves and their world from other perspectives. Whatever else it may be, the Christian gospel is not a secret lore but an open invitation.

In the first chapter, on theology and the God who loves, I look at some of the structuring elements of theology in selected areas of interpretation of the biblical narratives — talk of God's faithfulness in the Old Testament, New Testament accounts of God's engagement with human experience of life and death through Jesus, later work on the difficult but central notion of God taking death overcome into his own future activity as the triune God.

A chapter on the fundamental issue of love as a focus in theology leads to a consideration of faith, hope and love in

Christian tradition. There is an assessment of the advantages and disadvantages of the kind of theological integration pursued in the programme of love as focus, with comparative reference to aspects of the recent Continental work done on hope by Moltmann and Pannenberg and by Ebeling on faith. The development of the tradition on God's love is traced through a small group of selected themes, first in the patristic, medieval and reformation periods, and then in modern treatments.

Chapter six provides a transitional section in which the problems of the complexity of the human condition, to which the Gospel is addressed and for which theology is to be made comprehensible, are explored. Discussion of some perennial metaphysical and epistemological problems of Christian belief leads to grounds for a critical theology of love. The second half of the book, in the following seven chapters, represents an attempt to spell out in the exposition of doctrine some of the consequences of the concentration on God's love. Recommendations on specific features of the divine love, e.g. the relation of self-giving to self-affirmation and the results of ascribing this character to God as creator and redeemer, are applied to problems concerning the nature of God's agency, and to the development of Christology, as well as to the trinitarian problem and the question of the relation of theology to history. It is not claimed that definitive solutions have been achieved in a field involving a number of essentially contested concepts. But it is claimed that sufficient evidence has been produced to indicate that concentration on the love of God is a continuing source of fruitful development in the shaping of Christian doctrine, and that, applied to currently intractable problems, this approach enables us to take up the force of often unpalatable alternatives without masking the difficulties. The programme is then spelled out in a reconsideration of the doctrines of God, creation and redemption. Close attention is paid throughout to the analysis of different sorts of theological practice. I have long believed that it is in constructive dialogue with others that the ongoing work of the subject is most likely to be advanced.

It goes without saying that the reflections in this book owe much to the countless discussions of the love of God to be found in the history of Christian thought. In particular I want to mention two books which seem to me to be central to the subject. These are Daniel Day Williams' *The Spirit and the Forms of Love* and John McIntyre's *On the Love of God*. There is doubtless much more to be quarried than I have found. I hope to have been able at least to suggest that the theme is well worth pursuing further.

In writing this volume I have been indebted, consciously and unconsciously, to a great many people. Parts of this work, in various guises, have been tried out at various times in various places: I am particularly grateful for the comments of the members, past and present, of the graduate Christology seminar in this University. Anthony Baxter, Brian Hebblethwaite and Bill Shaw have produced invaluable comments on the manuscript. To all these people, and to my colleagues here and in Glasgow, especially Professor A. D. Galloway, my warm thanks are due. Lady Collins has supported me with endless patience and wise encouragement. I am grateful to Hazel and Gerald Hedge for the meticulous typing of this and my last book. My greatest debt is acknowledged in the dedication of this work to my wife.

George Newlands
Cambridge, March 1979

Chapter 1

Theology and the God who Loves

1

The belief that God is love is a central feature of the Christian gospel and a continuing source of strength and inspiration, often in the most trying of circumstances, to millions of people. This belief is not confined to Christians, though in the Christian tradition it has certain distinctive characteristics. At the same time, the statement that God is love is one of the most well worn cliches of recent times, often a platitude uttered as a substitute for any sort of constructive proposal in a particular situation.

In the past the response to inappropriate interpretations of theological affirmations has been to set the text in context, to tell the story of God's love as spelled out definitively in the biblical narratives, in the events to which they testified and in the doctrines which incorporated the results of reflection upon these narratives in the Christian tradition.

The urgent problems which press upon the theologian's task in the modern world have meant that this approach will not do any more. At least, it will not do by itself and as it was once conceived. For the Christian tradition is anything but self-explanatory to the majority of the world's population, which lives in societies that are either increasingly secularized or likely to become so in the near future. Familiarity with Christian life and worship is becoming the exception rather than the rule. Despite occasional phases of interest in religion of various sorts, it becomes increasingly difficult to think of our planet as created and nourished by the personal God of Christian faith. Indeed the ever-growing dimensions of the problems of poverty, hunger and man's inhumanity to man appear to make the classical ideas of God morally intolerable. It has sometimes been thought that if there is a God, responsible for such a world as ours, he must be a monster, and is certainly not to be worshipped. But in fact, the evidence suggests beyond all reasonable doubt that there is no such God. Atheism, practical or theoretical, has perhaps always been with us, but in our time the dimensions of the problem for the Christian have changed dramatically.

It is in this context that I want to reconsider a number of central issues in Christian doctrine, through a critical analysis of the basic affirmation that God is love. God is not an object in the world of objects. This has radical consequences for all aspects of theological explanation. Explanation in theology cannot be quite the same as explanation in carpentry.[1] But assertions without explanation remain incomprehensible. In any Christian theology there will remain large elements of residual mystery in speaking about the transcendent God. But we have a duty to explain as clearly as possible wherein the mystery lies. In a previous age theologians sometimes appeared to know too much about the personal details of the life of God. Today perhaps we theologians tend to identify with the agnosticism of the age and assure the reader that we are all in the same boat, and that none of us can say anything about God any more. But we should no doubt be rather at a loss if the same attitude to apparently intractable problems were taken by colleagues in other fields, say in the life sciences. We have to begin where we are.

2

Concentration on a single theme in theology is fraught with risks, but all intellectual activity is fraught with risks and makes progress by trial and error. Much theology, especially in the last two hundred years, since the Enlightenment, has been done with the aid of single motifs and concepts. These have been used to integrate discussion of a number of topics, in place of the older method of working through a number of traditional *loci* of doctrinal affirmations usually derived from the Apostles' Creed, or other creeds or confessional statements of the Churches. Naturally the choice of central motif has important consequences for the results obtained. These consequences are sometimes intended, sometimes unintended, and exhibit desirable and undesirable effects, depending on the criteria of assessment used.[2]

It is not necessary to entertain a strict view of 'the' one correct approach to doctrine in order to see that a great deal of talk of God has love has been superficial. There is a diffuseness, a sentimentality, a 'soft-centre' quality about much writing on the subject. Love as a major theme is absent, at least explicitly, from most of the best of recent Continental theology, though it has been prominent in much ephemeral production. Writers on the subject are not unaware of the difficulty. But still there is confusion of the particular issues of theology, the metaphysical, historical and moral issues, in a miasma of mind-blowing 'agapeomonism'.[3]

Talk of God is complex and there are perhaps almost as many concepts of God as there are users of the term 'God'. I want to show that exploration of the theme of God's love for us may help us to understand better a number of aspects of God-talk. As I understand the matter, the problems involved here are not necessarily greater than those connected with *any* sort of talk about the God of Christian faith. In so far as it is possible to speak of an essence of Christianity, it seems to me that the love of God is after all the essence or even the quintessence of Christianity.[4]

Theology as a discipline is today, in the last quarter of the twentieth century, in a somewhat untidy state. It would greatly sharpen up the issue for discussion if I were to assert that the only correct perspective from which to view the subject is as a theology of the love of God. The prospect is tempting. Writers on doctrine are rather given to producing large volumes without ever employing the word 'perhaps'. But clearly *the* way of speaking of God is reserved for the eschatological future. In this life our theologies are irrevocably pluralist. This does *not* mean that we cannot make recommendations about what are likely to be true and untrue propositions, or that there can be no criteria upon which to judge truth claims. We shall consider later the precise contribution of cultural relativity and of various sorts of relativism to theology. But it does mean that we cannot look at the issues from God's point of view.

I shall argue that there is indeed a way from God to man and from man to God, the way of Christ, well characterized by Karl Barth in his treatment of the journey of the prodigal son. Failure to give adequate weight to the substantive content of the Christian faith produces dismally tedious theology. But though faith is not without conceptual content, the way is, as I understand it, a way of effective and decisive salvation rather than definitive explanation. Barth could see this point, in theory if not always in practice. 'Dogma is an eschatological idea, to which each particular dogmatic statement is only an approximation, which can neither anticipate nor conceal it. . . . This door especially must not be bolted.' How it is possible without undue incoherence to argue for the reality of salvation while maintaining considerable epistemological scepticism will be considered in later chapters. I have long been struck by the aptness to our quest for dogmatic definition of Wittgenstein's comments on pontificals and highways.[5]

'A picture is conjured up which seems to fix the sense *unambiguously*. The actual use, compared with that suggested by the picture, seems like something muddied. Here again we get the same thing as in set theory; the form of the expression we use seems to have been designed for a god, who knows what we cannot know; he sees the whole of each of those infinite series and he sees into human consciousness. For us, of course, these forms of expression are like pontificals which we may put on, but cannot do much with, since we lack the effective power that would give these vestments meaning and purpose.

'In the actual use of expressions we make detours, we go by side-roads. We see the straight highway before us, but of course we cannot use it, because it is permanently closed.'

Talk of God as love can be diffuse. If we are to avoid un-clarity, then we must neither be afraid of using the word nor be bewitched by language as a substitute for substantive content. It is possible to say a great deal about humanity without using the word humanity, as say in some of Solzhey-nitsin's novels. The same is true of love. There are no magic words in theology, and no forbidden words: all depends on how they are used.

3

God, I want to suggest, is the one who loves, *par excellence*, whose nature it is to love. To understand God's nature as love is a major clue to learning how to use the word 'God', and to understanding the meaning of salvation. I shall set down at this point a brief, programmatic statement of the understanding of love that I shall be attempting to explain in detail in the succeeding chapters.

The first ground upon which I should want to argue that God is love is an interpretation of the biblical narrative. This is not yet, of course, an assertion that the Bible has any sort of metaphysical or epistemological priority, or even that we always come to think of Christian faith through reading the Bible. We may, but the question of the logical and theo-logical status of the Bible is anything but straightforward.

It is often said that in theology the choice of starting point is all important. Much more to the point, it seems to me, is the need to ensure that in the finished production all major

structuring elements are properly accounted for. I begin
with the biblical material because, whatever construction
one may later wish to put upon its logical status, this
material embodies most of the structuring elements of the
Christian tradition. What these elements are and why they
should be retained is a matter which we shall have to go into
in due course. I want to turn first to the substantive issues,
for I believe that in theology as in other disciplines,
methodological clarification may arise as much out of tack-
ling the material content of the subject as from attention to
method for its own sake.

Discovery of the implications of God understood as love
through reflection on the biblical narratives, which are
themselves a collection of widely varying and often conflicting records of different sorts of events, is by a slow and
cumulative process. God in the Old Testament is conceived
in an astonishing variety of imagery, but he remains always
the creator and sustainer of his creation, acting in providence, always with his people, looking after them in their
varied fortunes. All our own human experience, direct or indirect, is of service to us here in recognising the character of
God's concern, even where this may go beyond our expectations. At the same time, thinking about God as a transcendent, personal being who creates the universe and acts in
particular providence, suggests dimensions in God beyond
those which are the subject of our direct experience.

Love is a term which people have imported as a kind of
programmatic term to bring into shape and focus their
understanding of God's activity and character. Its content is
determined partly by our selection of particular parts of the
Bible, the tradition and our own experience for concentrated reflection. But our understanding of love is defined
too, by reference to what is taken to be the detailed particularity of the historical and the transhistorical activity of
God.

The supreme ground in the Christian tradition for a theological assertion of the centrality of the love of God has

always been an interpretation of the New Testament record
in terms of God's self-giving in the sacrifice of his son, and in
Jesus' self-giving to God and mankind. Here is the true
paradeigmatic structure of God's nature. The basis for this
interpretation is found in the force of the scriptural passages
in themselves, underlined through reflection on God's concern for men over the centuries as these themes have informed Christian experience. God is identified with his
creatures through his presence in Jesus, suffering, sharing in
life and death, sharing Jesus' lot, somehow even taking
death overcome into his own future activity as God.

Unity of love in this framework must be taken to be a
more inclusive, not less inclusive category than unity of
being. Such an interpretation of course goes well beyond the
biblical imagery in seeking theoretical understanding. It
raises difficult philosophical problems and requires discussion of the traditionally trinitarian implications of the
Christian faith. Such language is anything but self-
explanatory. But in seeking explanation we must be careful
not to explain the core of faith away, into something quite
different.

Jesus of Nazareth identified himself through his actions
with the lives and concerns of the people he met. At the
same time faith affirms that he was one with God in a way
which does not lend itself to exhaustive description based
upon empirical observation. The identification of God the
creator with his creatures reaches a climax in the death of
Jesus. Here the element of justice in God's love comes to the
fore, the need to act in such a way that his love is made
available to all men, however negative their reaction to God
may be. This action involves tragedy, as often in human life,
and the transcendence that may be involved in tragedy. But
however evocative of our devotion, tragedy is not and cannot
be the last word. In the resurrection the identification of the
cross is carried through to restoration and renewal. Self-
sacrifice is part of a larger and more comprehensive movement of self-giving which is grounded in and makes possible

God's love for all men. In human life self-giving may involve self-sacrifice to the point of destruction. So it does for God, as he participates in death, taking the awareness of abandonment into his own experience. But his purpose for mankind, reflecting the nature of his own being, is worked out in self-fulfilment, self-giving producing freedom.

The content of this self-giving is articulated in the foci of the public ministry of Jesus, in his teaching about the kingdom, and in later Pauline reflection on his life, death and resurrection, and Johannine reflection on Christ and discipleship.[6] (I shall not attempt to fill out the exegetical background. The manifold aspects of love in the biblical narratives appear to me to have been amply explored in the literature on the subject.)

God's self-giving enables people to give themselves to God and their fellow men without inhibition, destroying alienation from within; the opposite of the self-giving which imposes itself and creates alienation. It is important to see the resurrection as an integral part of this self-giving, though resurrection with self-giving would be mere triumphalism. God's love is an effective love, not an account of beautiful and tragic failure; this is the good news of salvation, apart from which Christian hope would be illusory.

The Christian hope is the hope of love. The grounds for this hope lie partly in reference to God's activity in the present. The manifold logic which leads faith to affirm the presence of God rests neither upon a private source of revelation nor upon a purely psychological condition. The affirmation of God's presence to all mankind, even where he is on occasion experienced as absent, arises from faith in the decisive realization of salvation through love in the events concerning Jesus. The presence of God, who was participated in death and shares the fruits of the resurrection through the Holy Spirit, is by definition not open to empirical observation, yet makes a difference to the empirical existence of those who have faith. They regard the hope of love as already fulfilled, even when only dimly perceived and hesitantly acknowledged, and far from perfectly under-stood.[7]

4

In providing suggestions about the nature of God and human destiny Christian faith at the same time raises a vast number of further questions. The above theological sketch is no exception. In particular it raises all the technical questions involved in what it is to perceive the transcendent, and of how God can be said to act. The problems too of the work of the New Testament historian must arise. At best we have perhaps made a start in saying something about the appropriate shape of the enquiry and the nature of the transcendent referent. Somewhat as in the case of other minds, the issues involved in the explanation of how we claim to know what we know are formidable. But concentration on the love of God as the focus of the relation between God, Christ, and mankind leads to a number of procedural considerations. Where the transcendent is intimately present to the world it is unlikely that theology or christology can be built up exclusively 'from above' or 'from below', not to mention 'from before'. It is unlikely to be profitable to attempt to use the accepted empirically based concepts of experience as the sole appropriate framework for theology. On the other hand, attempts to purify theological concepts in such a way as to remove them from the scrutiny of the rest of the human sciences are equally inappropriate. If our theology is to correspond more to astronomy than to astrology we can wave no magic wands. But if, as I believe, there is much more yet to be quarried from patient reflection upon the love of God, then perhaps we may find that we need none.

5

Let me pause to take account of what has just been done. I have tried to explain why the concept of love is important, and what sort of conceptual filling I have in mind, by setting love in the framework of what classical Christianity has usually regarded as being in some sense given, the tradition of the biblical narratives. It may be objected that in so doing I have begged the questions, presupposed the answers, and 'looked up the book' to find the authorized 'appropriate framework of reference' for my conclusions. My defence must be that the assertions made must stand or fall by the nature of the grounds on which they are to be justified.[8] This does not, of course, mean, as theologians have sometimes appeared to think, that the existence of God is proved or disproved by their arguments. I do not subscribe to the tough minded position that truth always lies in the extremes, and that these issues can only be discussed from strictly theistic or strictly non-theistic propositions. My concern is with the more fluid situation, which I believe to be ultimately more significant, in which at some times the strength of faith, and at other times the strength of doubt and perplexity, is most apparent.[9]

The message of Christianity is a gospel of faith, not doubt. Faith is central. It is intimately related to love and may be conceived of, despite the danger of fideism, as amounting to more than its component parts of belief, assent, commitment, entertainment of concepts and the like. Faith in God's providence is part of new creation. The gift of faith always lies before us. And since it involves an intimately personal though still mysterious relationship between God and men, it is open to all the contingency of human existence. There are some men and women who appear to lead untroubled, carefully planned lives with no accidents or surprises. There are those for whom the life of faith appears to be an unbroken, sometimes too unbroken path with no interruptions, byways, questions. But for most of us life is anything but an ordered, planned continuity. The dimension of faith participates in the variety of our experience and is illuminated, darkened and, we may hope, matured by our life in community. We need not make virtues out of order or disorder. But I shall argue that this openness of faith to vulnerability is no accident, but reflects the nature of God's love, constant in endless self-giving. We may not live in a circle of faith/doubt dialectic, characteristic of the thought of Martin Luther and to a lesser extent of Schleiermacher. We shall want to maintain the ultimate priority of faith. But the moving dynamic of faith, to use a much abused term, is not as irrelevant to our contemporary intellectual experience as we may sometimes imagine.

I have written about that which is in some sense given, in the tradition of the biblical narratives, and I shall have more to say about the complexity both of the given and the narratives. We may focus upon this element in many different ways. If we regard it as confined to the past, present or even the future all sorts of insoluble problems arise. We may regard it as fundamentally intractable, only expressible in highly imaginative imagery, ultimately opaque: in this case we shall produce results in the form of a 'problem'. We may classify it as a deposit indicated by capital letters, as Revelation, or Word, Word Event, or Holy Tradition: in this case too, the characterization will colour the treatment in significant ways. In the first instance, in speaking of the given in the tradition of the biblical narratives, I want to indicate simply that men believe themselves to have come to know something of God and his relation to men which they could not have discovered or deduced for themselves.

In speaking of a given element I do not regard this datum as self-interpreting or self-authenticating, or at least certainly not entirely so. Love is a word we use to a certain state of affairs, particularly in the biblical stories, but it is also a term through which we interpret the activity of God by comparision with human experience of and reasoning about love. It will help us in our quest to consider as wide a range as possible of human experience of love, and to examine the philosophical issues involved in the meaning and use of statements of what it is to love.

It may appear slightly odd to have spent so much time

already on the Christian tradition, after recognizing at the beginning of this chapter that the Christian tradition is anything but self-explanatory to the majority of the world's population. Christians need not however deduce that the increasing obscurity of their faith need detract in any way from its relevance. The eradication of personal freedom from a totalitarian state in no way undercuts the value of freedom. The opposite is the case. We shall not advance dialogue with non-Christians by ducking the central problems raised by our faith and sticking to peripheral and potentially less difficult issues. It is precisely by exposition, example and comparison that explanation may become effective and communication may take place. In the first instance, genuine communication often provokes tensions avoided in mutual disregard. That intellectual tension may be creative rather than destructive is a responsibility which we need to keep constantly before us.

Notes to Chapter 1

1 Explanation. cf. Toulmin, *Human Understanding, I*, (OUP 1972), esp. 41ff on the problem of conceptual change, also Edwards, *Encyclopaedia of Philosophy* (Macmillan, NY, 1967). s.v. Explanation (lit.) *Explanation* ed. S. Körner (Blackwell, Oxford, 1978).

2 Structures in textbooks. cf. Hoffmann, *Das systematische Lehrbuch*, on origins in Hellenistic Alexandria, and Grabmann, *Geschichte der Scholastischen Methode II*, 359ff. (Herder, Freiburg, 1909) on Peter Lombard, whose structure has long been influential, e.g. even on Tillich's S.T.

3 Aversion from love as centre stems partly from the Barthian critique of Ritschl. The antimetaphysical strain in Ritschl was, however, continued by Barth, Moltmann, etc., up to the work of Pannenberg.

4 For 'agapeomonism' I am indebted to S. W. Sykes. For recent

discussion of 'the essence' cf. J. Hick, *God and the Universe of Faiths* (Macmillan, London, 1973) 108ff., and S. W. Sykes in *Religious Studies*, Dec. 1971.

5 Wittgenstein, *Philosophical Investigations*, p.127e, Para 426 cf. Barth *Church Dogmatics* I.2.865. (Blackwell, Oxford, 1967).

6 cf. ch. 2-5.

7 cf. D. Stafford Clark, *Five Questions in Search of an Answer* (Collins, London, 1970).

8 As in Basil Mitchell, *The Justification of Religious Belief* (Macmillan, London, 1973).

9 cf. Peter Baelz, *The Forgotten Dream* (SCM Press, London, 1975); H. H. Price, *Belief* (Allen and Unwin, London, 1969).

Chapter 2

Love as Focus

1

Speculation without reference to specific examples is often rather hard to follow. I want to turn now to the focal concepts, and especially that of love, in the Christian understanding of God. God's love is often spoken of in comparison with human love for God. In medieval thought there is a standard practice of exegesis of the Bible in terms of the Pauline triad of faith, hope, and love, *fides*, *spes* and *caritas*. Love has gone, with the users of the term, through numerous cultural shifts, as courtly love, romantic love and so on. In theology and philosophy love has been articulated through all sorts of frameworks, existentialist, process and many others. A great deal of nonsense has been written about love in idealist frameworks and, like most modern writers, I prefer a version of a realist position. But this is not a simple choice which will guarantee results. For a great deal of nonsense has also been produced in realist frameworks, of various sorts. One has only to think of the follies of the realist opponents of Berengar of Tours, who forced him to assent to the proposition that in the Eucharist we crunch the actual flesh and bones of Jesus, or facile attempts to regard all uses of categories of substance as more ultimate than personal categories in talk of God.

The nature of love is not often considered in modern society as an intellectual problem in itself. More frequently it is related to the roles of sexuality in personal relationship, or to the realization of justice and economic growth in community, I want to begin however from love in a more traditional framework in the work of a writer on the threshold of the modern world. Love as focus is the key to John McLeod Campbell's *The Nature of the Atonement*, not well known but once described as 'the most systematic and masterly book on the work of Christ produced by a British theologian in the nineteenth century', and as 'certainly the most important English contribution to dogmatic theology made in the first sixty years of the nineteenth century'.[1] We shall not solve the problems of the present by appealing to the past, but a close look at Campbell's methods will serve our present purpose. The primary subject here is the understanding of atonement, but the atonement was to be taken always together with the incarnation, and the whole related immediately to the doctrine of God.

'Both Apostles' (Paul and John) see the love of God not in the incarnation simply, but in the incarnation as developed in the atonement. 'The atonement is to be seen as the action of God the loving Father. Divine forgiveness itself creates the gound of reconciliation between God and men. Human response to God's love is of course necessary, but the initiative remains with God.' (Here Campbell is both denying traditional theories of penal substitution, and refuting charges that he has reduced Christianity to deism.) God's justice is the justice of love. Reconciliation is an immensely costly process. God forgives and shows this in atonement. Atonement does not create the possibility of forgiveness. There is then no question of appeasing divine wrath through penal substitution. The forgiveness that is perfect justice, the love that abhors evil, works through Jesus' perfect repentance for the evil of the world as he suffers, a man among men and at the same time the son of the father. An atonement to make God gracious would be impossible: on the contrary, the scriptures 'represent the love of God as the cause, and the atonement as the effect'.

It is not then simply, as often in the tradition, in the death of Jesus, but also in his life that atonement is worked out. Orthodoxy had concentrated on Christ's sufferings as punishment, leading up to death as the judicial penalty for mortal sin. 'But my surprise is . . . that these sufferings being contemplated as an atonement for sin, the holiness and love taking the form of suffering should not be recognized as the atoning elements – the very essence and adequacy of the sacrifice for sin presented to our faith' (p.116). As love God participates in unloving humanity. Campbell chooses the biblical concept of fatherhood, qualified by other biblical imagery, to fill in the meaning of love. While stressing God's initiative, he has no hesitation in employing what he considers to be the best elements in human love in his theological construction. 'Living the life of love he must needs care for all humanity even as for himself; so being affected by the evil of the life of self, and enmity in humanity according to the life of love, and at once condemning that life of self, desiring its destruction, and feeling himself by love devoted to the work of delivering man from it, at whatever cost to himself' (p.127).

Wherever there is sin, estrangement from God, God's reaction is to suffer in his own nature. 'The full revelation of God is *not* that the divine love has been content thus to suffer, but that the suffering is the suffering of divine love suffering from our sins according to its own nature' (p.134). Jesus was able to make a confession of our sins while remaining sinless, because of 'a confidence connected with his own consciousness that *in humanity* he abode in his Father's love and in the light of his countenance' (p.175). In his ministry of identification and intercession, 'the outcoming of a life of Sonship', in the intensity of the agony of Gethsemane, the cost of reconciliation is spelled out. 'In truth, we are to judge that according as was the love which, in the strength of love to God and man was able to drink that cup, so also was the bitterness of that cup . . . The measure as well as the nature of Christ's sufferings is that of the divine love which experienced them' (p.264).

Contemplation of this drama through participation in the spirit of Christ brings about in us 'a movement of our inner being' an 'ascending upwards to the mind of God'. Again the image of the family: 'if we refuse to be in Christ the brothers of men, we cannot be in Christ the sons of God' (p.371). The reward of faith is the peace of God. 'Philosophy has been called a homesickness: the knowledge that in God we live and move and have our being is the conscious peace of home to our spirits when we know God as revealed in Christ'.

This all seems innocuous enough, but the ideas were once considered sufficiently dangerous for the Church of Scotland to expel its most distinguished theologian from its ministry and never to readmit him. More to our point, what if anything has this lengthy dip into a particularly tortuous example of Victorian literary prose to do with theology today? At one level, it may be said that Campbell's work was influential, though indirectly, and his ideas can be traced a century later in Donald Baillie's widely studied *God was in Christ*, published in 1948.[2]

Still, it would be difficult to underestimate the sweeping changes relevant to the task of the theologian which have occurred in the thirty years since then. The continuing development of the revolution associated with the name of analytical philosophy, the illumination of Christian tradition produced by application of historico-critical method, hermeneutical theory and the techniques of the human sciences, the development of modern society with its secular attitudes, science-based culture and social problems, the impact of Marxism and the fact of world poverty, these and other factors shape the environment in which we live and think. In such a period of accelerating change, of a whirlwind of change, it is not easy to think that anything from the past can help. But abandoning concepts of love in individual and social contexts is not likely to lead to a better future society. In looking to the future we may want to remember some of what has been learned in conflict and labour in the past.

The great strength of Campbell's thesis lies in the integral relation between incarnation and atonement and between the doctrines of God and of Christ. This was in principle a highly comprehensive theology, centred upon God's love and attempting to draw into the illumination of Christology the widest range of human experience. Campbell's explanations were not perfect. In rejecting what he rightly regarded as a crudely materialistic understanding of the efficacy of the death of Christ he stressed the spiritual nature of his suffering almost to the exclusion of their physical aspects, failing to take full account of the horror of the crucifixion and the depth of God's self-abandonment. In understanding consciousness as the hinge between the retrospective and prospective aspects of the work of Christ, its past and its effectiveness now, he telescopes some difficult problems. In speaking of God as the loving father he used images of family life with a facility at once illuminating and deceptively simple. But he understood that talk of the God of Christians always requires correlation to the person of Jesus, and to Jesus' understanding of God. Recently there has been an awareness of a distortion, associated with aspects of the 'dialectical theology' of estimates of the value of nineteenth-century theology. The appropriate response is not a return to the nostalgic enchantments of the past, but a theology which is unambiguously rooted in the present. If we are to do in our time what Campbell did for theology in his, we may expect the results to constitute a challenge and question rather than an echo of the conventional wisdom of the day.

2

I have looked at love as focus in a specific theologian. Now I want to look at a specific problem. In the light of the last section I can perhaps most usefully choose salvation. One central problem here, perhaps *the* central problem, is the relation of the events concerning Jesus to the present state of humanity. Whatever sets of categories we employ, there remain areas of unclarity. On the plane of historical research it is notoriously difficult to find any integral connection between events in the distant past and today's world. Jesus set an inspiring example. But there have been other examples, and examples will not produce theology except by gross inflation in the use of language. We may go on to assert that the resurrected Jesus is one in *being* with the Father, and that through his life, death and resurrection we are renewed in being in relation with our creator. But if we are not to become bogged down in yet another variation of the ancient discussion of the relation of being to becoming, being to non-being, we shall want to see being here as paradeigmatically instantiated in the love of God through Jesus Christ. This is not simply the love of Jesus who has died, but of God who has participated in death and now invites us to fullness of life, however we may come to understand this.

Secondly we can suggest that in Jesus the meaning of history is shown as the *history* (or perhaps *story*)³ of salvation, and go on to suggest that man may develop in mature historicality as he learns more of the God of history through the history of Jesus Christ. But the history of Jesus was as it was because men were as they were. The history of God involves suffering but is not normatively delineated by suffering. Further, we can only identify ourselves with one other completely at a given time, but God must rejoice with those who rejoice and suffer with those who suffer simultaneously. His participation is not only historical but transhistorical. Again, our projection of the transhistorical God must begin with the character of the particular events surrounding Jesus, the spelling out of the substantial content of love.

Thirdly we can say that in the events concerning Jesus the *Word* of God came to judgement for our sins and comes now to men as the word of grace, forgiveness, justification. The notion of the Word is itself of course complex. It sometimes seems that there are as many concepts of the Word as there are users of the term, and perhaps a few more. Stress is laid here on the place of communication in God's action. Jesus speaks, he teaches, he bears a message in his words and actions together. Salvation is of a certain sort and not another sort, and is not devoid of conceptual content. God's prophetic word cuts across the progress of history and refers both to the action of God and to the activity of Jesus. The Word is concretized in the loving activity of Jesus, of God towards Jesus and so towards mankind. In the events concerning Jesus, we may say, being, word and history are united in God's salvific participation in human life.

What difference does it make to stress the nature of this salvific participation as that of love? Why not simply say that in Jesus Christ God restores being, word, nature and history in an act of reconciliation? The justification, if any, will lie in our ability to offer a better explanation of the Christian understanding of salvation.

The other area to which I would like to refer now is the doctrine of God. I have maintained that the character of the Christian God is disclosed, especially in the life, death and resurrection of Jesus, as that of self-giving, self-affirming love. The love of God has a trinitarian structure (though by no means every trinitarian concept is satisfactory) in which unity of love includes unity of being, being which is involved in a constant process of complete self-giving which is also complete self-affirmation, in God himself and in his relations with the world. To use the traditional formulations, aseity is at the same time proseity, the economic and essential trinity are one.

3

I ought perhaps to raise here the question of what difference it may make in theology if we do *not* stress the love of God. I do not want to suggest that love is the only starting point in theology, but I would like to make one or two points in passing. Karl Barth is one of those who have spoken profoundly about the love of God. God's being is of the one who loves in freedom. It might be claimed that the whole of his theology was about the history of God's love for men, though not about the love of love in abstract. But it seems to me that a formal and explicitly articulated connection between God's love and God's grace, and God's love and his word, might have enabled him to avoid some of the well grounded criticism of positivism of revelation associated with Bonhoeffer,[4] and of verbalisation of the gospel associated with Pannenberg.

In Pannenberg's own Christology there is remarkably little of salvific value, of the reconciling love of God acting in atonement in Jesus. A similar gap is to be seen in Moltmann's *Theology of Hope*, where the problems of the present tend to be evacuated into the security of the future. In Barth the grace of God often appears to be so triumphant over the world of human experience as to be virtually incomprehensible. In more recent Anglo-Saxon theology, the world of human experience sometimes appears to be all, and the rules limiting God's behaviour are almost so strict as to rule him out of existence, not to say experience. Compromise between extremes is not a virtue. But exploration of the love of God, as I understand the matter, may enable us to discover new avenues of progress.

It would be foolish to suppose that there are not profound explorations of God's love in frameworks of theology which differ from mine. Theology is part of an ongoing communal activity of reflection, conversation and practice in which each is heavily dependent on the contributions of others. But it does seem to me that it is not enough to be able to say of a given theology that as Christian theology it is of course implicitly a theology of the love of God. If God *is* love, then this discovery has consequences at once radical and precise, and these must be constantly emphasized and reaffirmed.

Further, despite what has been said about 'revelational positivism', we may, I believe, come to see that the love of God as centre must affect all theology, the prolegomena as much as the substantive content. Here the preliminary questions are also basic questions. The exact nature of the relationships between God's love and our knowledge of him is anything but self-evidently simple. But the divine love is the centre, the only centre, upon which all our reflection should ultimately be focused.

A comparison between two classic approaches to theology may serve to illustrate briefly my understanding of the relation between concepts of love and the structures of theology. In the theology of Karl Barth, the love of God is implicit but only occasionally becomes the focus of conscious attention. In the work of Anders Nygren, there is painstaking and exhaustive analysis of all possible nuances of various concepts of love, in which God's love is understood to have a distinctive meaning in itself. I follow Barth in believing that God's love is to be understood from the particularity of the biblical narratives and the tradition of Christian reflection, and Nygren in believing that love must be articulated as the specific goal and source of this tradition. The disadvantage with Barth is that the dogmatic structure is always in danger of obscuring the reality of God's love. The danger with Nygren is that love may become a sort of 'ghost in the machine', a spiritual essence distilled out of etymology and intuition, lacking in rational, historical and theological grounds.

In this study I shall not attempt to cover the biblical and historical traditions in the manner of Nygren and many other writers cited in the notes. My purpose is to deal with the theological issues which have interested me particularly, and to draw attenion to the considerable literature which already exists, rather than to attempt a comprehensive replacement of what has been done. The theology practiced here will be rather different from that of the traditional biblical theology, based on concepts first in the Bible, then in doctrines of creation and redemption, characteristic of the Scandinavian Lutheran school in which so much important work on love has been done. In the fields of fundamental theology, the doctrine of God, creation and redemption, the suggestions are intended as much as a pointer to what already exists and urgently needs to be done, as an answer at this stage to the questions raised. In the field of ethics there already exists an excellent example of what seems to me to be required, in Gene Outka's admirable *Agape, an ethical analysis*.[5]

Notes to Chapter 2

1 On Campbell, cf. Storr, *The Development of English Theology*, 424 (Longman's, London, 1913), Pfleiderer, *The Development of Theology*, 382 (Macmillian, London, 1890), J. Macquarrie, in *Thinking about God*, 167ff. (SCM Press, London, 1975), and my chapter on C. in *Studies in 19th Century Theology*, ed. D. W. Hardy (forthcoming).

2 On Baillie, cf. my study of Campbell above (lit.): Baillie's work, though dated, seems to me to be important for Christology.

3 cf. Chapter 13 below, and E. Guttgeman's, *Offene Fragen zür Formgeschichte des Evangeliums* (Kaiser, Munich, 1970), esp. 237f. on Die Veranschaulichung des Kerugmas durch Erzählung.

4 cf. E. Bethge, *Dietrich Bonhoeffer* (Kaiser, Munich, 1967), and the writings of R. Gregor Smith, esp. *World Come of Age* (Collins, London, 1967) eds. R. G. Smith and J. A. Phillips, *The Form of Christ in the World* (Collins, London, 1967).

5 On love as a motif cf. e.g. Art. *Liebe* in PRE, Liebe in EKL and in LThK, *Love* in Hastings ERE 8, 160f., Agape in Kittel, *Theol. Dictionary of the New Testament*; J. Moffat, *Love in the New Testament* (Hodder & Stoughton, London, 1919); H.

Kuhn in *Phil. Rundschau* 3 on L in Barth, also, apart from G. Outka, *Agape* (Yale U.P., New Haven, 1972), *Nygren, Agape and Eros* (SPCK, London, 1957), etc., J. Cowburn SJ, *Love and the Person* (London, 1967); cf. too D. Z. Phillips, *The Christian Concept of Love,* in I. T. Ramsey (ed.) *Christian Ethics and Contemporary Philosophy* (SCM Press, London, 1966.) and J. R. Jones, Love as perception of meaning, in D. Z. Phillips (ed.) *Religious Understanding* (Blackwell Oxford, 1967). cf. CD Barth 2.2. 351f on God's love as grace. also CD 2.1 306ff. 755f, 764f, 1.1. 537f, 1.2. 371f, 4.2. 727f. and R. Prenter in ThLZ CP 33, June 1971 Der Gott, der Liebe ist. cf. too F. Herzog in Ev. Theol. 1968 2/3. also R. Hazo, *The Idea of Love* (E. A. Praeger, NY, 1967) cf. F. D. Maurice on the abyss of love in Theol. essays, 306, 316, 323. Schleiermacher cf. para. 9. pp. 167f. J. Macquarrie on love as 'letting be', *Principles of Christian Theology,* 310-11 (SCM Press, London, 1966). On the New Testament background of the workd of Spicq and Warnach on agape, and esp. G. Bornkamm on 1 Cor. 13, in *Das Ende des Gesetzes I* (Kaiser, Munich, 1966); faith, hope and love based on God's love. cf. too, on love and process, J. Cobb, *The Structure of Christian Existence,* 125f, *A Christian Natural Theology* (Westminster Press, Philadelphia, 1967) (Lutterworth London, 1966), and N. Pittenger, *Love is the Clue* (Mowbray, London, 1967). M. D'Arcy, *The Mind and Heart of Love* (Fontana, 1962). A. Ritschl, *Justification,* 276f., H. R. Mackintosh, *The Christian Apprehension of God,* 183f, V. H. Vanstone, *Love's Endeavour, Love's Expense* (DLT, London, 1977). P. C. Matheson, *Profile of Love* – Towards a theology of the Just Peace (Christian Journals Ltd, Belfast, 1979). H. Timm *Geist der Liebe* Gütersloher Verlagshaus Gütersloh, 1978).

Chapter 3

Faith, Hope and Love in Christian Tradition

1

'There are three things that last for ever: faith, hope and love, but the greatest of them all is love.' Separately and together, faith, hope and love have long been key categories for theological reflection. Faith has been a central theological motif particularly in the tradition of Luther and of modern existentialist thought. Hope has appeared as the new promise of a future orientated theology, with the prospect of dialogue with Marxism and participation in the changing of society. Love has come to the fore particularly in process thought in America.

There is an important tradition of interpretation of scripture and of theology as biblical theology, in terms of faith, hope and love. This goes back to Augustine and it dominated a great deal of medieval exegesis.[1] The reality of grace is shown in these three virtues, which appear as religious perfections of men. For Augustine, caritas is God's nature, not just an attribute.[2] For Thomas, God's love is the cause of our love for others, divine grace inspiring human initiative.[3] Peter Lombard stressed the interconnection and inseparability of the three theological virtues and, like Gabriel Biel, their relation to divine grace.[4] Bernard of Clairvaux explained their relationship in this way: *fides quidem illuminavit rationem, spes erexit memoriam, caritas vero purgavit voluntatem*.[5] From the traditional doctrine of grace as *habitus* Luther worked out his understanding of the special actual presence of grace in love. He could speak of God as 'a glowing oven full of love'. There is a close connection in Luther of faith and love. 'It is only in unity with *fides*, which understands itself through Christ, that the Holy Spirit grants life in love and frees from the law of sin and death.' Hope too is related to faith, and so is transformed from the natural expectations of human nature to a distinctively Christian hope in God and his actions. Faith has for Luther its ground not in itself but in God's justification through Christ.[6] Again it is the doctrinal context in which these motifs are set that gives them their distinctive meanings in various stages in the tradition. I want to take the unfolding of this process a stage further by looking at the separate used of faith, hope and love in recent theological construction.

2

Faith and unfaith, belief and unbelief, these are standard terms of response to the Christian gospel recorded in the New Testament. Faith has been a central term in articulation of response to the gospel since earliest times. In doctrine the locus *De fide* is standard, appearing in various places in the systematic structures and related to other *loci* in various ways. Since the Reformation justification by faith has been *the* central doctrine in the Lutheran tradition.[7] Sometimes theological traditions have spoken of the nature of belief rather than of faith, and often the emphasis has subtly changed. But faith, variously defined, has played an important role in all theology. As human response to the gift of the Holy Spirit it has been understood in innumerable different ways.

Typical modern Lutheran accounts of faith can be seen in the work of Rudolf Bultmann and Gerhard Ebeling. Here faith is expressed largely in concepts derived from existentialism. The results have advantages and disadvantages, some of which derive from the existential component rather than the concept of faith as such. Faith in Reformation theology was often divided into three components of fiducia, assensus and notitia: here the element of fiducia predominates. Faith is trust, often despite all appearances and sometimes even to the extent of making notitia, historical or other information, and assensus, an act based on rational grounds, unnecessary.

Reflection on faith may help to ensure that theology is not reduced to a shallow rationalism or empiricism. It may also guard against unthinking acceptance of the dogmatic authority of traditional formulas, and even the belief that God somehow puts us in possession of the sort of knowledge of him that Christians hope to have at the end of time. Theology is done *in via*, is always provisional and subject to correction.

But concentration on faith is at the same time subject to the dangers of fideism and voluntarism, unreasoning faith which sees theology as simply a leap in the dark. Here openness to receive new insights is replaced by an unwillingness to consider arguments and grounds for and against belief. This is a danger but not an inevitability, and arises when preoccupation with faith obscures other structuring elements in theology. Understanding of faith may be aided by dialogue with doubt, understanding of belief by exploration of relations with unbelief, and the sort of area indicated by half-belief.

Jesus himself, according to Gerhard Ebeling, made much use of the term 'faith' in his teaching. Seven times in the synoptic gospels there is the phrase 'your faith has saved you'. The earthly Jesus himself, rather than say the cross and the resurrection, makes possible and gives faith. Jesus gives faith, which lends certainty and meaning to man's existence. Jesus is not only the object, but the ground and source of faith; this faith comes from Jesus' own faith. The wider task of Christology then consists in amplifying what 'came to expression' in the earthly Jesus. We can say nothing of Jesus which is not grounded in the Jesus of history, and nothing which goes beyond saying who this Jesus of history is. He is the primary object of devotion. Post-Easter faith knew itself to be nothing other than the true understanding of the pre-Easter Jesus. The medium of continuity between the pre-Easter Jesus and the post-Easter Christ is a speech event or language event. What comes to expression in the language event is the only true reality for theology.

Against this solution, it may be argued that the historical Jesus is, historically speaking, almost unrecognisable to us. Käsemann has suggested that it is unlikely that the earthly Jesus spoke of faith, for faith did not belong to the historical situation of the Jesus of history. To project the later situation on to the earlier is historical anachronism. The belief that the historical Jesus is the basis of faith is then left as a sort of dogmatic intuition, as it was for Herrmann, writing at the end of the nineteenth century. We may conclude that the relation of faith to theology and christology in particular involves a wider complex than understanding the historico-critical method, and the hermeneutics of dealing with written texts. If it implies statements about the way the world is, then we are involved in metaphysics, and correlation with the methods of the natural perhaps as well as the human sciences. If the world is not merely to be understood but to be altered, and we are invited as Christians to participate in a new order, then we must seek to assist in this change, according to the will of God, if we can hope to discern this.

3

Sometimes it is said that theology ought not to deal with abstract and speculative questions about the nature of God, the possibility of there being a God, the details of obscure doctrines or even the individual's understanding of historicality and transcendence, but should look at the concrete problems of this world now in the light of the Christian hope. An excellent example of this perspective is to be seen in Jürgen Moltmann's *Theology of Hope*. It is claimed that concentration on this world's problems arises from the theological centre of faith itself when properly understood. Christianity's basic theme is not faith, knowledge, revelation or mystical illumination but promise, promise of God's future for all men. Hence the theme, theology of hope. We should cease to be preoccupied with the present, its problems and uncertainties, and begin instead to look at the world with a set of priorities based on our knowledge of God's promise for the future of his creation. Hope puts the problems of theology into a completely new perspective.

At a time when the very different dialectical theologies of Barth and Bultmann appeared to have lost impetus, Moltmann struck a new note. Hope stresses the positive side of the gospel, rather than the doubts and the problems of interpretation. A link is forged in a fresh way between doctrine and ethics, between faith and action, Church and society, the gospel and social change.

We must begin from the discrepancy between theory and reality in the rediscovery of the category of the eschatological in twentieth-century theology. 'The eschatological is not just a part of Christianity, but it is precisely the centre of the Christian faith, the tone which affects all else.' The God of hope is 'a God with future as his essential nature'. It follows that the person who hopes in Christ can no longer be satisfied with reality as it is given. Peace with God implies dissatisfaction with the world. 'The God of exodus and resurrection "is" not eternal presence, but he promises his presence and nearness to him who follows his summons into the future.'

The essential simplicity of the case in no way detracts from the brilliance with which it is built up. The great insight of the dialectical theology was its eschatological emphasis, yet the significance of the discovery was never fully exploited. 'The thought forms in which the real language of eschatology is still hidden today are throughout the thought forms of the Greek spirit, which experiences the eternal presence of being in the logos of epiphany and finds there the truth. (Even where modern thought is indebted to Kant, this concept of truth still remains.) But Israel found the truth of God, not in the logos of the epiphany of the eternal present, but in the word of promise which is the basis of hope.'[8]

There are difficulties in Moltmann's account, especially in the areas of philosophical complexity, questions of truth and interpretation, metaphysics and epistemology. In addition he tends to play off Hebrew thought against Greek, and to exaggerate the elements of Platonism in areas of Christian tradition from which he wants to differ. The exegetical evidence for the massive use of the category of promise leaves much to be desired. Some of the inspiration for the conclusions comes not, as indicated, simply from the biblical narratives, but from his earlier work on seventeenth-century Reformed orthodoxy; acknowledgment of this inspiration might actually have strengthened his case.

The basic structural category is then promise, which 'binds man to the future and opens up for him an appreciation of history'. Through the culmination of promise in apocalyptic, 'the whole world, and not just the world of men and peoples, comes into God's eschatological judgement of history'. It might be thought however that promise is not the only category which leads to an appreciation of history, and that the interpretation promise-apocalyptic-history is just one of many useful axes of Old Testament thought.

Yet illuminating theological suggestions have been made before through exegetical special pleading, as in the writings of Karl Barth. All depends on the specific instance. We must turn now to the working out of the category of hope in particular theological issues. Moltmann began with

Christology. Despite his replies to critics, his New Testament exegesis is clearly as it were preprogrammed. All exegesis has pre-suppositions. The difficulty is to judge how strictly our models may be applied. Of the theological tradition it is said that for the Reformers the gospel is virtually identical with promise. Central is the interpretation of the resurrection of Jesus. 'We recognize historical phenomena in their own historicality only when we perceive their meaning for their future. In this sense the event of the resurrection of Jesus from the dead is an event which can *only* [my italics] be understood in the category of promise.' The consequences are a new Christian understanding of history and of mission, the necessary relation of which to the New Testament discussion is unclear. 'The centre of the New Testament scriptures is the future of the resurrected Christ, which they announce, point to and promise.' But it might be thought that the centre includes also confession of past experience of God and thanksgiving for his present presence or nearness. It is in the social and political sphere that Moltmann, in the line of Althusius and others in the Reformed tradition in the seventeenth century, interprets his thesis with the most radical effect. The present is suspect, the future is all-important. 'Eschatology of the present means nothing other than creative expectation, hope that sets about criticism and changing of the present, because it lays itself open to the universal future of the Kingdom.' Whatever our views of political issues (and I have personally a great deal of sympathy for Moltmann's position) it is difficult to see the 'changing of the present' can be an adequate translation of the practical essence of the gospel. As in the case of faith, concentration on hope will not in itself solve the problems of theology, though it may be a useful instrument to be used along with others.

4

It is tempting to draw the conclusion at this point that it is likely to be less profitable to move from a category like hope (or faith or love) to a theme such as God or Christ, than to move from these terms to faith or love. But we may not suppose that we already have an exhaustive knowledge of God, or God in Christ, as a key. In understanding of all our terms there is a balance of known and unknown elements. We must reluctantly conclude that Moltmann's programme will not do, or at any rate it will not do all that is claimed for it. But not all is loss. Concentration on a particular theme has produced striking, imaginative suggestions, which are none the less useful even when they illuminate only part of the whole picture. The critique in particular of aspects of theological tradition and Christian attitudes is suggestive even where it is imprecise.

It may be of course that the difficulties involved in a given account, e.g. in the theology of hope, are due to methods used by the writer which are not due directly to the central motif.[6] Certainly the same particular strengths and particular weeknesses occur in Moltmann's next book, the profound but in many ways deeply unsatisfactory account of Christology in *The Crucified God*. Here again the observations on substantive issues of Christology are often acute, but the treatment of metaphysical and epistemological issues is very slight. It may then be, not that 'motif' studies are inherently unsatisfactory, but that all depends on the treatment of particular issues in each case. Reference here to general methodology will be rather like talk of the famous ghost in the machine, and equally obscure.

Following on the work of Moltmann, Panneberg and others there has been consideration of a new theology based on an 'ontological priority of the future'. Both the New Testament and Christian tradition have also spoken howewer of the nearness of God in the present, and of the crucial significance of God's activity in the past. At different periods in history stress has been laid variously on past, present and future; the relation of God to time is not resolved by stressing one dimension at the expense of the others. In Molt-

mann's later work, to which we shall return, the significance
of past and present are given great weight. *The Crucified
God* develops the implications again of a single basic theme,
'the cross of Christ as the foundation and criticism of Christian theology', and the strength of the book lies in the
powerful assertion of aspects of substantive issues of faith,
particularly the involvement of God in human death in the
crucifixion of Jesus.[10]

5

We have already spoken about concepts of love in the nearer
and more distant past, from Augustine to McLeod Campbell. For Peter Lombard love was the bond of relationship,
the essence of the Holy Spirit. Love was the central feature
of Abelard's understanding of the work of Christ, and also of
Thomas' Christology. Talk of God's love for us and our love
for God were thought to illuminate one another in the
characteristically subtle treatment of nature and grace in
the tradition of St Thomas. In the Christian Middle Ages all
analogies from human love were to be pursued as far as
possible in seeking to understand God's love, allowing for a
careful distinction between creator and creature but not
disallowing a careful doctrine of analogy. The concepts of
human love utilized naturally reflected the changing
patterns of cultural understandings of love – courtly and
romantic love, love in a filial or paternal sense, love involving sexuality, love as social concern in different frameworks of society, feudal, paternalistic and totalitarian. The
history of Western literary thought about love has been well
brought out by a number of writers, notable by Roger Hazo
in *The Idea of Love*, in which he analyses the tradition from
Abelard to Rousselot and other modern writers. The
varieties of thought about human love for God in theology
are excellently set out in Gene Outka's *Agape*, in which

attempts to play off *eros* against *agape*, Greek thought against Hebrew, classically in Nygren's *Agape and Eros* but in many other writers since, are analysed.[11]

In modern systematic theology, there is a sense in which the whole of Karl Barth's *Church Dogmatics* might be described as a theology of the love of God, in that it is concerned with the activity of God on behalf of man though Jesus Christ. I want to look here at the specific references to God's love in paragraphs 18.2 and 28.3 (my translations, as throughout unless indicated):

'Love is the nature of the Christian life. If there is nothing in Christian life that precedes love, yet God's love to man must have preceded Christian life, so that this could now really begin with love. The love of God is poured into our hearts through the Holy Spirit, which is given to us (Romans 5.5). It follows from the fact that God is love, not that we ought to love, but that we can and must love. The self giving of God in his son is precisely the love of God towards us. God is love, before and apart from his love to us. He is, like all that he is, as the triune God in himself. It is then actually God's free mercy and goodness that we encounter in his love.' Four points are worthy of special note. Barth insists on the intimacy of relation between our love for God and God's love for us. He indicates the connection between the love of God and the Holy Spirit. He interprets love in relation to the life and fate of Jesus of Nazareth. He speaks of God's love as the essence of his being, a trinitarian nature of mutual love.

In a later and pivotal section of his doctrine of God Barth elaborates on the fourth point. The paragraph is on God's being as the one who loves (para. 28.2). He is in this manner God, therein lies the deity of God, that he loves; and this is his love, that he seeks and creates fellowship with us. Precisely this loving is God's being in time and eternity. 'God is' means 'God loves'. This is the ultimate meaning of what it is to be a person. 'Actually and originally, to be a person means to be what God is, that is, to be loving in the way that God is loving.' Further, 'the one, the person whom we really know as a human person, is the person of Jesus Christ. This one man is indeed the being of God which makes itself known as the one who loves'.[2]

Barth failed to develop fully the consequences of this understanding of God's love. Sometimes God comes through his work as a sort of objectified construct of self-related being, and this concept of God has produced some particularly arid theological fruits. It is possible to imagine a more fruitful approach through Barth, with the aid of Schleiermacher and others who might have found the combination strange, to the problems raised by the Enlightenment for the Christian doctrine of God. We shall attempt to understand the loving God as the ever present subject, in whom consciousness of those whom he has willed to sustain in creation is itself a feature of his own subjectivity. Such a conception of God through Barth's work would represent not the rejection but the affirmation and deepening of the nineteenth century quest for a more adequate understanding of God in the modern world.

One may note here that though the minutiae of difference in theological positions remain as crucial to theological progress as minutiae in microbiology, the development particularly of comparative studies in religion throws light on the enormous similarities in Christian theologies. Invocation of a methodological 'principle of charity', which has nothing to do with compromise theology (Vermittlungstheologie) can lead to breaking down inhibitions in the development of traditionally opposed doctrinal concepts. Such inhibitions have of course strong cultural and ecclesiological as well as intellectual springs.

Barth's concern has been echoed, in quite different ways and usually without direct reference to the passages quoted above, by a number of later writers. Ernst Fuchs has attempted to understand the being of God as love through analysis of the actions of Jesus as activities of loving behaviour.[13] These activities are understood as having a kerugmatic value, proclaiming the nature of God directly,

and are in this way distinguished from the ethical understanding of God in the nineteenth-century work of Albrecht
Ritschl. As we have mentioned, Jürgen Moltmann understands God's being distinctively characterized in the suffering love of the cross, in death and its overcoming. Eberhard
Jüngel, a pupil of Barth and Fuchs, has combined the ideas
of God as self-related trinitarian being with the notion of
God as overcoming death through the cross of Jesus. The
same spelling out of love in relation to the cross is seen in the
Scandinavian Lutheran tradition in some of the work of
Regin Prenter. 'God's love becomes visible in the events
which occur in Jesus' death, when he dies for the godless, for
his enemies, when the father does not spare the son but gives
him for us all in his death and resurrection. That is the love
of God.' In both Barth and Prenter the emphasis on the
loving God remains implicit rather than explicit. We can
only speculate on what they might have produced in a programmatic expansion of these passages.[14]

6

Mention has already been made of Albrecht Ritschl, whose
impact on Barth has always seemed to me to have been
rather greater than Barth himself was ever inclined to allow.
But I want to turn now to a rather different area from the
Continental theme, and look at the work on the love of God
in America, associated with Norman Pittenger and especially D. D. Williams, which borrows much of its philosophical assistance from process concepts. Pittenger's work
tends to suffer from its own special virtue. It attempts quite
rightly to widen the concept of love to embrace the most
catholic of sympathies. The difficulty is that when concepts
become universal it is hard to pinpoint their specific applications. But his books are full of imaginative imagery,
especially on the ethical dimensions of love. In attempting

to preserve the fragile structure of an open society we can only disregard 'old-fashioned liberalism' in development of Christian love at our peril.

More weighty in respect of the doctrinal implications of the theme of love is, in my experience, the treatment of love in D. D. Williams' *The Spirit and the Forms of Love*. Williams offers an excellent survey of the biblical background to concepts of God's love, and then an analysis of three forms of love in Christian tradition – the Augustinian, based on the unchangeability of God, the Franciscan, centred on personal dedication and the search for poverty of spirit, and the Evangelical, built on the understanding of God's love as the grace of forgiveness. He criticises the metaphysical tradition in Augustine for seeing perfection in immutability, proposes a metaphysical alternative in response to a new historical consciousness, and finds this in process thought. The relations of God, man and salvation are then articulated through a new structure of five categories of love – in individuality, freedom, action and suffering, causality and impartial judgement in concern for the other. The love of God the creator brings salvation to men through the self-sacrifice of Jesus. The implications of salvation for life in contemporary society are worked through in excellent chapters on love and sexuality, love and social justice, love as non-violent protest, and love and intellectual endeavour. I rather suspect that Williams could have said all that he wanted to say about the importance of God's involvement in historical contingency without the process framework, but the framework has in this case undoubtedly helped him to explore the detailed implications of God's self-involvement in reconciliation.

If it is true to say that in Barth's early Christology there is a strong tendency to emphasise the Person of Christ at the expense of his Work and in Ritschl a tendency, not perhaps as strong as is usually imagined, to stress work rather than person, Williams is an example of an approach based on a different philosophical framework, in which neither incarnational nor soteriological considerations are allowed to predominate. My approach is in some ways similar, though I am unable to place the same confidence in one particular philosophical tradition. Certainly we cannot have Christ without his benefits, as the traditional phrase expressed matters, nor benefits without his person. We must have both, despite the difficulties of the Christological given. We look for some sort of articulation of Calvin's *Christus cum beneficiis suis indutus*. We shall have to speak of parables, models, symbols, but we will have to try to bear in mind that our technical devices may easily mask as many problems as they help us to disclose. Perhaps nowhere more than in theological methodology is it easy for us to confuse our programmes with results.

It emerges from considerations of faith, hope and love that examination of the primary words can never be enough. I hope to have indicated that there may be advantages in making reference to the love of God explicit rather than implicit. But the strength of our constructions will lie more in their ability to elucidate more adequately problems inherent in the substantive issues of theology than in their assistance in developing pictures, however suggestive in themselves, based on the word 'love'. I want to turn now to some of these basic issues which press most upon adequate explanation at the present time. Though the exposition of a complete systematic theology is beyond the scope of this book, we shall have to deal, one way or another, with most of the central areas of Christian theology. 'It is characteristic of fundamentals that they cannot be treated in isolation from one another.'[15]

Notes to Chapter 3

1　cf. the excellent study by R. Schwarz, *Fides, Spes und Caritas beim jungen Luther* (Berlin, 1962) ARG 34.

2 For Augustine cf. J. Burnaby, *Amor Dei* (Hodder & Stoughton, London, 1937) cf. esp. De Trin. 15.17.27.

3 On Thomas cf. U. Kuhn (Göttingen, 1965) *Via Caritatis* esp. ST 1920 on the love of God. O. Pesch, *Theologie der Rechtfertigung bei Martin Luther und Thomas von Aquinas* (Mainz, 1967).

4 For Peter Lombard cf. M. Grabmann, op. cit., and on Gabriel Biel cf. H. Obermann, *The Harvest of Medieval Theology*, Eerdmann, Michigan, 1963. *Caritas et gratia sunt inseperabilia* (Biel), cf. Schwarz 105f.

5 De. Div. Sens. 45. For Bernard of Clairvaux cf. Grabmann, op. cit. II, 104f, and Outka. On Richard of St. Victor cf. De Trin. 3.3 on caritas (cf. Nygren 646ff) cf. P. Rousselot, *Pour l'Histoire de l'Amour en Moyen Age* (Münster, 1908).

6 For Luther on faith cf. Ebeling, *The Nature of Christian Faith* (Collins, London, 1961), Luther, and *Evangelische Evangelienauslagung* (Fontana, London, 1972), also Holl, *Luther*, (Darmstadt, 1962) in relation to Christology esp. still H. J. Iwand, *Rechtfertigung und Christusglaube* (Kaiser, Munich, 1966), also B. Gerrish, *Grace and Reason* (OUP, 1962), B. Lohse, *Ratio und Fides* (Vandenhoek and Rupprecht, Göttingen, 1967), and G. Rupp, *The Righteousness of God* (Hodder & Stoughton, London, 1953), and W. Joest, *Ontologie der Person bei Luther*. Luther's language about God's love is derived from the medieval image of the crucible. cf. the exx, cited below, ch.11,n.10. Of the fourth evangelist he comments '*Denn er sagt nicht, Gott sei das höchste Gut, sondern er sei dei Liebe*' – in contrast with much medieval theology. For Aristotle God is not in the first instance love.

7 For the faith motif as centre cf. Ebeling, op. cit. and *Word and Faith* (SCM Press, London, 1963) esp. pp.201ff, Käsemann esp., *Jesus Means Freedom* (SCM Press, London, 1969) passim, W. Herrmann, *The Communion of the Christian with God* (Williams Norgate, London, 1895), and R. Bultmann, cf. esp., *Commentary on the Fourth Gospel*, esp. on Jn. 15.4, and Marburger Predigten (Tübingen 1956). On Bultmann (Göttingen, 1964), cf. I. Henderson, RB, (London 1965), G. Hasenhuttl, *RB and RB in Catholic Thought*, ed. O'Meara and Weisser (Herder, NY, 1968). On Christology

and hermeneutics, esp. with ref. to Gadamer, cf. my *Hilary of Poitiers*, op. cit., 115f, 176f.

8 On Moltmann on hope cf. my review in Epworth Review Sept. 1976, 119-20.

9 For hope as a central motif cf. *Hope and the Future of Man*, ed. E. H. Cousins (Fortress, Philadelphia, 1972), *History and Hope*, by J. Pieper (Burnes & Oates, London, 1969), *Well-founded Hope*, by H. Berkhof (John Knox Press, Virginia, 1969), E. Bloch, *Das Prinzip Hoffnung* I-III, R. W. Jenson, *The Knowledge of Things Hoped For* (New York, 1969).

10 cf. Moltmann, *The Crucified God* (SCM Press, London, 1974) cf. my review in Theology, March 1975, 148f.

11 cf. Outka, op. cit. passim.

12 Barth, C.D. 1.2. 371ff (= K.D.I.2. 408ff) and C.D.II.1. 272ff (= K.D.II.1.306ff). On Barth cf. H. Frei in *Faith and Ethics*. (Harper & Row, NY, 1965) ed. P. Ramsey, pp.99-115, and my review of Eberhard Busch, *Karl Barth* in JTS April 1978 (SCM Press, London, 1976).

13 d. Fuchs, *Studies of the Historical Jesus* (SCM Press, London, 1964) and Festschrift for E.F. ed. Ebeling, Jüngel and Schunack. For F. the history of Jesus is the history of the power of love, cf. the Festschrift, esp. Jüngel, pp.193ff, and Ibid., *Death; The Trinity – God's Being is in Becoming*, and *Gottals Geheimnis der Welt*.

14 Prenter, op. cit. TLZ 1971 and *Creation and Redemption*.

15 G.H. v. Wright, *Time, Change and Contradiction*, 15.

Chapter 4

God's Love and Human Understanding

1

Theology is produced for human beings by human beings. It can only use human words, and these are deeply inadequate for speaking of God. We cannot see God as he himself does for he is transcendent, even if he is also immanent. Of God in himself we know nothing, except in so far as God gives this knowledge to us. In seeking rational grounds for our faith we may deduce various probabilities which may count for and against a cosmos-explaining being, but more we cannot say. If we have any grounds for believing that we have some knowledge from God himself, then this information has had to be adapted to the limitations of our minds, if it is to be intelligible to us. It need not conform completely to our previous conceptual expectations. It may lead us on from the realm of the familiar to the realm of the unfamiliar. But if there is to be genuine communication there must be some sort of analogical relationship between God and our language about him. There could be an exception to this, if God were to implant in us a miraculous capacity for understanding a new and strange conceptuality. But such evidence as the Christian tradition affords suggests that this sort of mechanical relationship is precisely not the nature of God's ways with men.[1]

We are dealing with human language, and with a richly

manifold variety of ways of speaking of the love of God. In so far as the Christian faith points to ways in which God's love transcends ours, we may expect to be led to a more profound understanding of love, human and divine, from our own partial and limited conceptions. We cannot expect to understand God's love the more by simply neglecting to consider the wealth of human understanding of love both joyful and sad. To do full justice to the issues of understanding, love and God would require at this stage a full scale study in the philosphical issues themselves. But neglect of these questions produces inevitable defects — a notable case is Emil Brunner's treatment of God's love. We shall opt for the method of introducing the appropriate analyses as they arise in the course of the treatment of the doctrinal themes.

There have been a number of excellent studies on the history of concepts of love and their scope and variety in the present, in sociological, psychological and philosophical contexts, not to speak of the resources of literature. I have learned most from Gene Outka's splendid *Agape*. All of the human sciences, and in important respects also the natural sciences, shed light on an activity so characteristically human. Love and hate are two of the central fibres of so much that men have done. The most obvious point to make here is that whatever we mean in speaking of love, we intend always to speak of the activities of personal agents. Machines do not love one another, unless they have been programmed to operate in a manner imitative of human beings. To speak of God too as the loving God is to speak of God as characteristically a personal agent. The dimension of the transcendent will lead us to expect that such a concept must be qualified. We need not imagine that we can play off love against being, activity against ontology and the like. But though the God who loves must clearly be more than a personal agent like human agents, he cannot easily be understood to be less than this. This brings us at once into a number of difficult problems about the meaning and reference of language about God, and the structure of the metaphorical terms we employ. What is it to speak of the God who acts, and how does he act? Does he act in separate, contingent, particular, historical events, or is such a conception of the relation of the transcendent God to the world a kind of 'category mistake'? How is the model, to use an overworked word, of personal agency to be understood? A personal agent reflects, intends, carries out his intentions in action. He is a centre of consciousness, whatever that may be. This raises endless problems for talk of God, who is clearly not an object in the world of objects, however pre-eminent, and not an embodied self, at least not in any sense common to our talk of other selves. What this personal agent could be like, how we could know what he is like and how he could communicate directly with us, are anything but easily answered questions. The various conflicting answers given in modern theology to these questions are evidence, not of wilful espousal of heretical opinions, but of the genuine difficulty of the problems. Whether or not the specific proposals made in the following chapters are constructive will depend largely on their ability to take account of this dimension.

2

We have said that it is possible to say a great deal about a subject like humanity or love without ever using the primary word, and this has often been done by great novelists. Something has been said of the texture of God's love, of ultimate concern, providential care, reconciling grace, without speaking specifically of love. Some of the greatest crimes have been committed in the name of love. Focus on love has served to draw attention away from precisely those issues with which one might consider the love of God to be concerned — love without justice in many societies in history.

In speaking of love we may have a thousand different

things in mind. None of them may be irrelevant to the understanding of God's love. Inevitably we shall decide that some areas are more central than others. The grounds upon which we decide and the criteria we use will come from the particular, in this case theological, issues with which we are concerned. The same is true in assessments of human love. The sorts of expressions of love that strike us as essential to a loving relationship between two individuals are rather different from those which appear significant in speaking of the love of governments for the social welfare of their electorates.

Despite the differences there are also important underlying similarities. This makes it possible to produce ethical frameworks in which certain recommendations, however informally stated, remain persistent elements. These include, for most people, respect for persons and non-exploitation of others. They imply further recommendations about equality of opportunity, about justice defined in certain ways and not in other ways.

In the modern world love is spelled out characteristically with reference to terminology of involvement, concern, commitment, identification, responsibility. It is characterized by self-giving, not as an end in itself but as ultimately self-affirming, as action with a view to human fulfilment. Such an understanding presupposes a great many other things. It involves a rejection of evil and of all that is opposed to love even where that rejection may have to take the form of choosing the lesser of two evils. The existence of certain types of evil counts of course against the love of God. It implies an understanding of goals for human existence, however provisionally described. It involves the capacity and desire to attain the maximum possible information upon which to base love which is appropriately directed. Misdirected benevolence often exasperates affliction. It implies the existence of a certain sort of personal agency, in God's case agency which is able to be directed simultaneously in a number of different directions to immense tasks. It implies possibilities of communication, of response and of developing mutual relationship between the parties involved.

The ways in which we speak of the love of God will always be influenced greatly by the concepts of deity which we recommend, and by the concepts of action, communication and response which then emerge. These in turn are shaped by our choice of frameworks among accounts of the relations, for Christianity, between creation and redemption, and by the extent to which theology is open to the issues raised since the Enlightenment by historical, scientific, sociological, political and many other disciplines. Generalizations are always disappointing. But attempts to particularize by ignoring important areas of the subject are equally doomed to futility.

3

In rejecting the notion of knowledge of God through direct miraculous implantation by God we have implied certain concepts of God and man, concepts indicated in chapter one. Ideally we ought to discuss all aspects of theology, methods, concepts, doctrinal affirmations, exhaustively in relation to one another at every stage in our discussion. This is the method employed by Barth in his *Church Dogmatics*. It has the great merit that none of the implications of one theme for another are left unexplored. The disadvantage is the obvious one of length and repetition. It is however with specific reference to the implications of love that I shall consider concepts of deity precisely in relation to human understanding in this chapter and in relation to creation and redemption in the following chapters.

4

In speaking of human understanding in relation to God's love it is desirable to make explicit, as briefly as possible, the understanding of the methods, norms and criteria of theology with which I am working. Most theologians, asked about criteria, will speak of reason, revelation and experience. With these I would concur. The distinctive characteristics of particular theologies are shown in the particular way in which these norms are handled.

Because God is love, he gives himself to men in love, and is to be loved in response. This does not invalidate the exercise of reason. With St Thomas I take it that religion may go beyond the realm of human reason, may need to be explored with the help of revelation, but is not contrary to reason. Reason is not automatically the ally of religion and raises formidable questions. But this whole study is built up on the understanding of belief in God as love as the unfolding of a cumulative rational case. It is important to avoid the sort of reductionism in which concepts of God are made to conform to arbitrarily and narrowly drawn criteria of coherence which rule out both transcendence and revelation. But the 'foolishness of the cross' need not lead us to revel in contradiction and luxuriate in muddle described as paradox and mystification venerated as mystery. This would be ethically and intellectually intolerable. If Kierkegaard was right in drawing attention to the role of the leap of faith in theology, then this must surely be a leap in the light rather than a leap in the dark. Critical rationality remains a *sine qua non*.

In speaking of revelation in the light of what has just been said, it is clear that there must always be a considerable overlap between reason, revelation and experience. We cannot be content, as Luther was, to leave reason to the things of this world, and refuse to apply critical reasoning to concepts of revelation. It may well be, as we shall see later, that revelation is not a primary word in theology like say salvation, and we shall see that there are severe problems with recent theologies of revelation. But in the informal sense of indicating that Christians claim to be able to make affirmations about God, notably as the God who loves, which they could not have discovered for themselves by reasoning from non-theistic to theisic data, revelation is involved.[2] Such affirmations are based, as above, in the first instance on the critical interpretation of the biblical narratives, though these are understood in the tradition of Christian experience through the Church.

The question of the appropriate role of the Bible in theological construction is exceedingly complex. My own usage throughout this study is frankly dependent on decisions based on my understanding of theology as a whole.[3] This in turn is related back to the biblical narratives: such a process is a hermeneutical circle: whether it is an increasing circle which produces deepening illumination or a vicious circle resulting in increasing self-deception depends entirely on how the resulting theological constructions are judged.

I take it as read that the Bible is neither the vehicle of a self-authenticating Word of God, nor a mere repository of historical information. History will produce, and ought to produce, nothing but history, and should not be turned into instant theology. In what areas then lie the indispensable elements of the Bible for theology? I find the following essential elements. First, certain historical affirmations relating to data involving the people of Israel, the life, words and fate of Jesus, and the early Christian communities. Secondly certain basic theological affirmations, referring to what have been described as 'relational centres' of the Bible, including the love of God, Jesus as the Christ, the kingdom of God, the death and resurrection of Jesus, the presence of God. The understanding of God's salvation through Jesus remains the central task of Christian theology.

It seems to me to be important to note that the early communities not only shaped the data about Jesus but were themselves decisively influenced by the historical events in which Jesus was involved, as well as by the theological affirmations which he made and which were made by the communities themselves. In a somewhat similar way, it is not enough for contemporary Christian communities to decide what constitutes for them the essential gospel. Unless they themselves are decisively influenced by external criteria then the claims of Christian faith become almost impossible to justify. If we can and do speak of some parts of the Churches' traditions as being one-sided in relation to the gospel, then we must operate and in fact continue to operate with some sort of scriptural norm. This norm is of course no guarantee that we will automatically make the right theological decisions. All our decisions, whether based on scripture or on tradition, inevitably reflect the provisionality of the present as present, as well as its eschatological limitation.

I have argued elsewhere that the ideas of scripture as self-interpreting, and of the Word or revelation as self-authenticating, despite their honourable tradition in theology, are in no sense an exact or authoritative explanation of the communication between God and man. This does not mean however that the tradition of God's word becomes useless, or that 'word' need always be replaced by 'history' in an almost identical role. The biblical record, too remains of central significance, if theology is not to turn into mere truism or groundless speculation.

5

The third area involved in criteria is experience. Experience has not always been a fashionable word in theology, but is clearly indispensable, and intimately related to all reason and revelation. All our knowledge comes to us through experience, direct or indirect. Revelation in the Bible and the Church is channelled through experience. But experience is a term which embraces the widest possible range of meanings. Experience that is illuminating is not experience of experience, but experience of something else. In theology, the question is always, experience of what, and what sort of experience? Appeal to experience is nothing like appeal to a single invariable entity.[4]

When Christians speak of the love of God they claim that God's loving care is confirmed from personal experience. God is not an object in the world of objects, and anything or anyone experienced as such an object is clearly not God. This elementary fact is often mentioned and its consequences are just as often overlooked. Yet such is the power of pragmatist and empirical criteria that we often use such criteria in our appeal to experience in theology. There is one *particula veri* here. If belief in God makes no empirical difference to the lives of Christians, then this counts against the truth of Christian claims about God. A God who is so inconsequential is scarcely worthy of serious consideration. But it does not follow that we need to postulate an empirical object (again a theory-laden description) in order to make an empirical difference. Here theology usually speaks of the many dimensions of the doctrine of grace. We shall have more to say of experience in speaking of the God who loves as man's creator, as redeemer and as reconciler through his Spirit.

6

The issue of criteria for truth in theology as in philosophy is not easy. 'Common sense' since the Enlightenment quite naturally expects truth in any sphere to depend on meaningfulness, meaningfulness involving correspondence to facts in the world of natural events. This has implications for the relation of theology to secularization, and for the understanding of God's action. We cannot simply deplore the modern consciousness. But as in philosophy, so in theology common sense may not be the best guide to analytic judgement. Indeed, since we have affirmed that God is not simply an object in the world of objects, the truth of claims about

God can never be decided on such a basis. We are involved inevitably in metaphysics. A flight from metaphysics is characteristic of modern Protestant theology, especially in the development of soteriology with an epistemological basis. But it is desirable in theology to attempt to characterize the object of faith in other ways than simply in terms of the ways in which it can be known.

This is not a simple or clear-cut issue. If it was Schleiermacher's misfortune to attempt to close the gap between truth and intelligibility by characterizing God in terms of the manner of our knowing him, it was also his genius. To feel dependent is to have knowledge of God. For Barth, on the other hand, God is hidden to men and is available only through grace which creates faith. The nature of God in his revelation itself imposes limits on our concepts. The concept of 'God' is to be filled out through his revelation in Jesus Christ.

I agree with Barth in opting for a realist attitude to truth which is not however a naïve realist attitude, i.e. which does not expect truth to be identical to meaningfulness seen in terms of correspondence to facts in the natural world. But such an approach to truth, pursued further, could lead in turn to the discarding of some of the features of Barth's theology and a renewed appreciation of aspects of the work of Schleiermacher. Focus upon Jesus Christ, a man in history who may be studied through all the tools of the human sciences, and at the same time God incarnate, is not the end but the beginning of a highly complex task to which there is no single key in the solution of any particular outstanding issue. It is singularly unfortunate that much theology especially in Britain in the last hundred years has thought it necessary to make a clear choice: either Schleiermacher or Barth. Creative theology comes from new combinations rather than standing in entrenched positions.

On the issue of truth conditions, the great advantage of Barth is that God is to be seen not in terms of his acceptability to us but as he gives himself in revelation. This can be accepted, and the question still raised as to whether Barth's interpretation of the details of the revelation, the all important filling out of the given, is correct. Barth too has his epistemology of revelation, in terms of self-authenticating event. We have asked whether this is the best interpretation of the biblical narrative, whether God is given to use solely through the biblical revelation, or also through the reflecting and worshipping tradition, the experience of the presence of Christ now. For God whose nature is to give himself in incarnation, in, with and under the human response to himself, it might be thought that reference to events in the empirical world is not entirely irrelevant theologically, provided that such reference is seen as an inclusive rather than an exclusive restraint.

Barth reinterprets talks of God as talk of Jesus Christ. But presumably a realist reinterpretation could begin with God the creator, or God the Holy Spirit just as well as with Christology: we shall examine an interpretation of God as Spirit later. What matters is not the starting point of procedure of a theology but its faithfulness to the Gospel. Still, Barth's emphasis on the need to avoid the constrictions of prior conditions remains important in speaking of truth in theology.

Notes to Chapter 4

1 R. W. Hepburn, *Christianity and Paradox* (Watts, London, 1958), W. Pannenberg, *Revelation as History* (Macmillan, N.Y., 1968), F. Ferre, *Logic, Language and God* (London, 1962) and R. H. King, *The Meaning of God* (SCM Press, London, 1974), also Walsh, *Metaphysics* (Hutchinson, London, 1966) and G. F. Woods, 'Doctrinal Criticism' in *Prospect for Theology*, ed. H. H. Farmer (Nisbet, London, 1966). cf. too J. Hick's excellent *Evil and the God of Love* (Macmillan, 1966).

2 cf. I. M. Crombie in Flew & McIntyre (eds.) *New Essays in Philosophical Theology* (SCM Press, London, 1955) and in Basil Mitchell (ed.) *Faith and Logic* (Allen and Unwin, London, 1957). Also T. Penelhum, *Problems of Religious Knowledge* (Macmillan, London, 1971), esp. 108f on 'probative revelatory phenomena', and I. T. Ramsey, *Religious Language* (SCM Press, London, 1959).

3 On the Bible in Theology, cf. the chapter on the role of the Bible in contemporary theology, in my *Hilary of Poitiers* (Peter Lang, Berne, 1978), pp.169-99 also J. Barr in JR Jan. 1976, and P. Stuhlmacher, *Hermeneutics and the Theological Interpretation of Scripture* (Fortress Press, Philadelphia, 1977) and G. Ebeling in ZTh.K, March, 1978. On this whole issue I have long been indebted to the writings and the encouragement of Professor James Barr.

4 cf. Chapter 12 below, and J. M. Hinton, *Experiences* (OUP, 1973).

5 Light has been thrown on the complexity of the relations of truth, meaning and reference in recent philosophy by the work of Dummett, Davidson and others. cf. M. Dummett, *Frege* (Duckworth, London, 1973); 584ff, Original Sinn, and What is a Theory of Meaning? II in *Truth and Meaning*, Essays in Semantics, ed. G. Evans and J. McDowell (OUP, 1974), also A. Millar's excellent thesis, *Realism and Understanding* (Ph.D.Cambs, 1974) and *Ibid*, Mind, 1977, 405f. cf. too J. R. Heal, What is a theory of meaning? Mind, April 1978, and C. J. R. Wright in PAS 50 Sup. 76, 217f. This discussion may seem a long way from the love of God, but is in principle entirely relevant. If we are to speak of God's love, we are committed to God's love as truth. On method in general, cf. Lonergan, *Method in Theology* (DLT, London, 1971) 'Method is not a set of rules to be followed meticulously by a dolt. It is a framework for collaborative creativity', cf. P. T. Forsyth's valid but dangerous maxim 'we cannot wait for knowledge till we have a satisfactory epistemology to license it', *The Principle of Authority*, 101 (Hodder & Stoughton, London, 1910), or more recently S. Kripke, 'Mathematical quantification is no substitute for philosophy', Evans and McDowell, Ibid, 416.

Chapter 5

Towards a Critical
Theology of Love

1

In this chapter I want to explore further the nature of theological method, and in particular through analysis of two contrasting proposals, the relations between theological methods and practices and those pursued in other disciplines, in the human and natural sciences. Theology, as response to the love of God towards men, should, we have said, be 'neither parasitic upon nor isolated from other academic disciplines, disciplines with in the first instance theoretical, but also practical applications.

I want first to take a look at the largest recent study in this field, Wolfhart Pannenberg's *Theology and the Philosophy of Science.*

The implications of concentration on God's love for the development of systematic theology will be examined. Neither a 'strict' system developed on deliberately exclusive epistemological principles, nor the system of the non-system, which has itself an inner compulsion, classically exemplified in T. W. Adorno's *Negative Dialektik,*[1] nor a general ecclecticism appear to me to be in any way self-evidently correct. At the same time I ought to attempt to spell out the way in which I myself attempt to work, not as another exclusive option but as a matter of personal recommendation. It is my concern, and I believe this to correspond, at least in an informal sense, with my understanding of God's love, to articulate a theology, which is neither reductionist in the pejorative sense of omitting central elements of the Christian gospel, not exclusive in attempting to maintain a single preferred and pure stream of orthodox doctrine, sharply distinguished from all perspectives. Theologians, like politicians, are wont to speak of openness, freedom and at the same time correctness as privileges peculiar to their own views. They often refuse to listen to other points of view, and then believe that others have nothing to say. Such attitudes destroy the value to society of the theologies they seek to safeguard. I want at least to be conscious of these issues and to seek to relate God's love quite specifically to the problem of theological methods and structures.

2

When we consider the fundamental issues of theological method, we turn instinctively not to British and American or African theology but to Continental Europe. Barth and Bultmann, Rahner and Tillich, Moltmann and Pannenberg: these are the scholars, perhaps, who have made the greatest impact upon the study of theology throughout the world in the last fifty years. All were born, educated, and did most of their seminal thinking on the European mainland. With the partial exception of Tillich, German was the language of their creative thinking. We may regret the imbalance, propose to ourselves other names, but there it is. When we come to look for explanations of this Continental fluency, one source is obviously the presence of an unbroken tradition of intensive theological scholarship through sundry reformations and enlightenments to the present time. Another source must be the continuing relationship between the theological tradition and the continental tradition of philosophy. Without this relationship none of the above mentioned writers can be understood, and none could have written as he did. It is often remarked that continental theology has been heavily indebted (too heavily indebted) to the philosophical tradition of the human sciences in the last couple of hundred years, whereas Anglo-Saxon theology has owed more to the methods of the natural sciences. The former has been more idealist, the latter more realist and empiricist, the former more given to metaphysics, ontology and sweeping generalization, the latter disinclined to general conclusions, more interested in epistemology than in metaphysics. By and large, though practice is much less tidy than theory, the global characterisations fit.

That is why *Theology and the Philosophy of Science* is such a promising and exciting project.[2] A theology which succeeded in taking critical and creative account of the fruits both of the Continental and Anglo-Saxon philosophical traditions, and of the methods of the human and the natural sciences, would be an enormously useful resource. The complex problems involved are unlikely to yield to the first assaults, and Pannenberg appears to me to have placed all his successors considerably in his debt.

Over the past five years there have appeared a number of German studies of the relationships between theology and philosophical method, of which this is probably the most significant.[3] Pannenberg deals first with the relation between scientific method and theology. Here as elsewhere there is a fluctuation between *Wissenschaftstheorie* meaning philosophical method in general, the distinctively scientific character of philosophical method, and reference to the particular contributions made by the philosophy of the natural sciences, which does not make for clarity. But the central concern is clear. Faith and reason are not irreconcilable opposites, but faith as the basis of the theological enterprise is inherently rational. Theology is never a leap in the dark.

3

Pannenberg embarks on a critical examination of work in

philosophy in the manner of 'logical positivism'. Positivism becomes an umbrella term which covers the theological positivism of Barth and Bultmann and leads, by reference to Kuhn and Hempel, to the relation of theories of falsification to historical methodology. Great stress is laid on the argument that 'philosophical assertions are always about reality as a whole, whether it is all the aspects of a single phenomenon or the whole of reality as the semantic context of every individual phenomenon'. Here we are back to the characteristic concern for the totality of reality which is in the background of much of Pannenberg's thought. In his work on theological anthropology he had succeeded in bringing together the most widely assorted data from the biological and anthropological sciences under the general term of historicality. But rather as in anthropology one scholar's profundity appears often to be another scholar's truism. I suspect that here the concentration upon essence and totality is itself much less absolute, much more theory-laden and liable to revision, than the author allows for. Despite the informed discussion of the work of the 'Vienna Circle' earlier in the chapter, I fear the problems on its agenda have been 'overcome' rather too swiftly.

We come now to the philosophy of the social sciences. Discussions of Weber, Habermas and others produce the thesis that 'sociological theories of action are always dependent on semantic constructions, which in turn are related to the totality of meaning which constitutes the horizon of any human grouping's experience'. Detailed consideration of Troeltsch and of theories of explanation and understanding leads to the conclusion that the differences between such theories relate 'not to the explanatory process in itself, but to the methods used in the different disciplines to produce explanations': I am reminded here of Käsemann's constant protest against what he regardes as 'artificial harmonizations' in New Testament scholarship. If you look for syntheses and totalities you will surely find them, and you are entitled to stick to them. But you have a critical duty to

weigh your preferred explanation against alternative accounts of the data at every point. For all the commitment to
historicality and contingency, this project suffers somewhat
under the compulsion of the system of the non-system.

At the end of this section the art of hermeneutic is traced
from origins in ancient Greece. (For all the apparent precision, the origins could be traced with equal plausibility in
half a dozen other Greek sources – perhaps a salutary
thought.) Against Gadamer stress is laid on the importance
of an element of objectification as a fundamental structural
element of language. I wish the theological implications of
this point had been pursued further, if only to note the
residual intellectual untidiness of the subject matter of
Christian theology. Examination of truth and meaning in
Habermas and Frege leads to the not now unexpected proposals that 'in the all-encompassing totality of meaning,
therefore, meaning and truth coincide', and 'it may be
assumed in advance that the situation in theology will prove
to be similar'. It is not entirely clear to me what it is, on this
account, for meaning and truth to coincide, and I am
mildly hesitant about theologies in which talk of God is so
strictly preprogrammed.

4

Against Schleiermacher's understanding of theology as the
science of Christianity it is now asserted that theology can do
justice to Christianity only if it is a science of God. As a
science of God its subject matter is reality as a whole, even
though as yet uncompleted whole, of the semantic network
of experience. As for Barth, the critical question is 'whether
he has succeeded in making God and his revelation anything
but the postulate of our (or his) consciousness'. Assertions
about the scientific status of theology on grounds of ap-
propriateness to its object (Torrance) are to be regarded
with great caution. Of theology it is concluded that 'though
it considers everything that it studies in particular relation to

the reality of God, it is not a positive specialized science. The investigation of God as the all-determining reality involves all reality'.

'God is the object of theology only as a problem, not as established fact.' Still, 'if God is to be understood as the all-determining reality, everything must be shown to be determined by this reality and to be ultimately unintelligible without it' (302). There are a number of interesting generalizations here. I could scarcely imagine myself commenting that 'modern philosophy is totally dominated by the Augustinian idea that man cannot understand himself in his relation to the world without presupposing God as both his own origin and the origin of his world'. Through further consideration of the scientific status of theology a cumulative case is built up for justification of the talk of God, with grounds for and against. The criteria are however pretty wide. Where everything is everything nothing is anything – though that would be an excessively uncharitable interpretation of this programme. Pannenberg's work has achieved an important breakthrough beyond a certain impasse in the Christocentric theologies of Barth and Bultmann, and one can scarcely complain of a lack of concern for Christology in the author of the splendidly comprehensive *Jesus, God and Man.* At the same time, as I understand the matter the events concerning Jesus do have important implications for fundamental theology as well as for dogmatic theology, and omission from this chapter of the Christological dimension serves to underline a concentration upon the epistemological rather than the metaphysical foundations of theology, perhaps parallel to a notable lack of stress on salvific values in the Christological study. Stress on rationality in theology is most certainly necessary, but perhaps not entirely sufficient.

Pannenberg finally sets out his own understanding of a science of religion as theology of religion, with appropriate roles for the various branches of theology. The distinctive nature of Christianity is 'the working out of the historical consequences which have flowed from the basic tension of Jesus' proclamation of the Kingdom of God and are constantly rekindled from it'. This leads to practical theology, which is obliged 'to explore the general truth of the unity of God and man in Jesus of Nazareth and of the presence of the coming Kingdom in him, as a hope for mankind and the basis of the Church's practice' (440).

'Theological science' is a magnificent theme, but its exponents are eminently prone to plunging irretrievably into theological nonsense. The higher they fly, the further they fall. It can be said at once of this programme that it contains anything but nonsense. Here we have a cool, sane and thorough discussion of the whole field of the nature of rationality in the foundations of theology. For my part I remain less than convinced by many of the arguments. Despite the subtle nature of the discussion of theories of meaning, truth and knowledge, I am not sure that the sheer difficulty of making general statements about the nature of the whole of reality of a sort which gather up the detailed results of widely diverse sorts of philosophical discussion, not least in the philosophy of science has been appreciated. As far as theology is concerned, the almost exclusive attention to epistemological considerations makes Pannenberg *qua* theologian disappointing, as Moltmann though philosophically unsophisticated by comparison is exciting. Again though the fashion in 'death of God' theology has passed, to be replaced perhaps by the death of Christology in turn, the issues raised by the phenomenon of secularisation will not go away. After all, it is perfectly possible to embrace theories of transcendent values as the clues to all reality without appeal to an external divine transcendent referent. Millions of highly intelligent people find no grounds for believing in God, and they do not believe.

5

A contrast to this framework, strikingly illuminating for our purpose, can be seen in another work specifically entitled *Theological Science* by T. F. Torrance.[4] This is a thoroughly contemporary account of what contemporary theology should be about and it is most instructive.

This is an essay in the philosophy of the science of God. What is required of us here is not a Philosophy of Religion in which religion is substituted in the place of God, but a Philosophy of Theology in which we are directly engaged with knowledge of the Reality of God and not just with religious phenomenality.

In such a context, science and metascience are required not because God is a problem but because we are. Scientific theology is active engagement in that cognitive relation to God in obedience to the demands of his reality and self-giving.

How God *can* be known must be determined from first to last by the way in which he actually *is* known, (a reversal here, as in Luther, of the Aristotelian custom of argument from possibility to actuality). Knowledge of God is knowledge in the proper sense of the word, involving a conscious relation to an object which we recognize to be distinct from ourselves and it is conceptual, the auditory rather than the visual aspect of conceptuality being very important. The actuality of knowledge of God is located in Jesus Christ, is given, given from beyond our own consciousness, is fact which has objective ontological reality, is not lent but is the self-communication of the Word of God. God reverses or converts our whole relation of knowing, in directing it out beyond all possibility in ourselves to knowledge of God, altering the shape of our minds to receive and recognize the truth.

Believing in the reliability of the Creator theology has sown the seeds of modern science. Concentration upon the word of God upon the self utterance of the truth, and the acknowledgement of its absolute primacy, cut the strings of prejudice and prejudgement and determined theological procedure, confounding Augustinians, Romans, Lutherans,

Kant, Schleiermacher and all other misguided thinkers. So too natural theology may offer the greatest hindrance to natural science and to scientific theology alike.

But what is scientific activity? This is the rigorous extension of our basic rationality, as we seek to act towards things in ways appropriate to their own natures, to understand them through letting them shine in their own light. Scientific activity searches for elemental form, moving from the many to the one, the complex to the simple. In theology this means openness to the logic of grace, allowing God's word to shape our knowing in conformity to him so that we may know the truth.

Truth as we know it consists in the conformity of things to their reason in the eternal word of God, so that the truth of every created thing is evident only in the light of God himself.

6

What is the relation between these theological thought forms and other forms of rational activity? In theology, whenever our knowledge of the truth is properly ordered it will reveal a structure in its material content that reflects the Christological pattern of the hypostatic union: This is the interior logic of theological thought. Knowledge of the Truth of God demands relation to the Truth in time and action that is a verbal relation, one described by verbs and adverbs. Knowledge of the truth requires a decision, an act of obedience on our part but this obedience is already there in the hypostatic union. Further, our natural language is rooted in being, and may be divided into existence statements (the logic of which requires interrogation of our concepts to provide constant reconstruction in terms for theology or correspondence to the word and act of God through the *analogia fidei*), and into coherence statements, which can be ordered together in open-ended systems with the aid of Gödel and God. In theology it is by relation to the Incarnation that our statements have their fundamental ontologic cf. Mark 4 in the light of Frege. This must involve a powerful element of apocalyptic, that is epistemologically speaking, an eschatological suspension of logical form in order to keep our thoughts ever open to what is radically new. It should also supply those operating in the other sciences with sufficient conceptual content to guide their recognition of the divine realities.

Because of the incarnation, historical science has a special relation to theological science; the incarnation has a special inherent rationality, as being unlike any other historical event known to us. It requires an act of discernment. This is what we call faith, i.e., the adaptation of the reason given to it in the process of acknowledging God's revelation in history and of obedient response to the Word of God communicated in human form (*pace* Bultmann). So Jesus insists on being understood in ways that will not submit to our historical criteria. Dogmatic statements involve propositional relations with God as the absolute subject and propositional relations between the human subjects within the covenanted community. However, it is the human nature of Jesus Christ that becomes the norm that we must use in determining the form of dogmatic statements as they are correlated to the human subject as well as correlated to the divine subject. As such, Dogmatics stand or fall with respect for the majesty of God in his word and for the transcendence of his truth over all our statements about it.

7

The merits of this approach are considerable and should be self-evident. Here is theology written with confidence, at a time when many theologies are dying of self-generated embarrassment at their own existence. The breadth of knowledge and depth of intellectual capacity involved are self-evident and impressive. It is indeed as if a traveller, journeying through the wasteland of modern theological suburbia, picking his way between the decaying rows of existentialist semi-detached here, and the vulgar pockets of Wittgensteinian prefabs there, were suddenly to light on a fairyland castle in a clearing, stonebuilt, solid, enormous and yet elegant, bewitching and dazzling. A fortress of the faith.

Yet I fear that if our traveller were to enter this fortress, slipping in perhaps by a side door, he might soon be sadly bewildered. For as he steps in, some of the paving stones on the floor seem to make an odd creaking sound. It is the discovery of the biblical and Hebrew distinction between creator and creation which forms the source and the clue to the nature of modern science. Why should it then be that the Hebrew people were more backward than all their neighbours in the ancient world in the development of science? There may be a proper explanation and correlation, but the stone no longer seems as immutably firm as before. Gödel's theorem helps us to understand the nature of translogical steps and relations between different levels of logic, showing too how the structure of a formal system, by its very nature, must be open: this is useful for the exegesis of the Bible, e.g., Mark 4, not to speak of showing us the structure of incarnational ontologic. But, as is clear to readers of, for example, the *British Journal of the Philosophy of Science*, the exact significance of Gödel's work is a matter of continuing debate on a wide front.

The biblical exegesis is difficult. 'Considered from the point of view of theological enquiry, the parable (parabole) is the concrete form which Jesus throws (ballein) alongside of or parallel to (para) his Word in order to bring it to bear upon our understanding and to apply it to our actual human life' (275).

Much of the material on logic, on natural science, and on

theological methods in general appears to be firm enough. But not all the firm stones are at the foundation of the pile.

Down among the foundations our traveller fares even worse than before. What is appropriate objectivity in theology? What is the object of our study? What sort of faith does theological science serve and how? Is the object of theology the Word of God himself? Or is it rather the multiplex sources of Christian faith? Are these two the same? Is faith simply rational assent, 'the fidelity of human reasoning to what is actually there in the encounter, the personal presence and act of God in our human and historical existence'? (325). Is this Stoic and Aristotelian sunkatathesis an adequate way of understanding faith? For the Reformers themselves, after all, faith was seen as containing the elements of notitia, assensu and fiducia. That is to say, it is a complex process with multiple strands, which cannot be pinned down in the given of God's alleged self-revelation. Notitia involves historical information, given in the story of an historical community, witnesses too in the several strands of historical documents.

Faith involves assensus, consent to the conclusion which the church has drawn from this information. But assensus, for the Church and for its members, is closely tied together with fiducia, with the awareness of being drawn, with the people of the tradition, in all ages to God himself. This is in no sense a compulsion, a forced decision.

8

Whatever grace may be, I have no evidence that it need involve a compelling logic which schematises my thinking. Grace, indeed, is always the grace of God in Jesus Christ: but the story of the grace of God is the story of the love of God in human terms, of one who stands at the door and knocks. In this portrait of God as one who thinks only certain types of pure thoughts in certain pure ways, whose sons must have good habits and tidy minds, who will only allow us to think of him in one prescribed way, and flies from the human sciences, I believe it is possible to see signs of a consistent anthropomorphism of the very kind that is theoretically avoided. If we must have anthropomorphism – and clearly we must – then let it be as near to the pattern of Jesus of Nazareth as possible, even where this leaves us with uncertainty in faith.

It seems to me that if God's love is indeed known a posteriori, that is, from experience of God's love, then the way is open to asking all sorts of further questions which are usually asked about human experience, if faith, which is human faith, is to understand itself.

As with faith, so with theology. I believe it is no longer possible in an ecumenical age to imagine that only Calvinism has the sole clue to the absolute truth of being: yet Torrance comes very near to saying this. Purism here, obsession with finding a single way and seeing all in terms of this way, may well be a great hindrance to awareness of the varied insights of the various traditions.

As far as understanding of the nature of historical judgement and historical development is concerned, this approach appears to offer little that Origen could not have said. To dismiss the intellectual tradition of the humanities in Europe over the last 200 years in this way seems to do little honour to God's creation.[5]

The God of logic and of physics appears here strangely remote from the familiar issues of human life, of suffering and tragedy, living and dying, human relationships and emotions. To exalt the majesty of the Word so as to stress to the full the perversion of man is not necessarily always a form of spiritual humility.

It becomes clear that methodological purity is not enough. If as I understand it the object with which theology has to do is in fact a multiplex object, then the scientific response to it (and response is itself only one of a number of images each of which has a limited usefulness) will also be multiplex in character. There are no magic words, no elixir of theological truth, for theology, to continue the image, is nearer to chemistry than alchemy. How to understand the objectivity of God whom faith confesses in terms of the relativity of faith's confession, how to understand the word of grace in terms of the love expressed in incarnation which is the content of the word, how to combine the ecumenical tradition with the universitas of the academic disciplines in order to make full use of the tools available, and at the same time produce detailed studies in small specific problem areas of theology – seeing details in terms of the horizons and then from more detailed precision broadening the horizons, would appear to be part of the exercise required. But inspiration will not come from beyond. Each of us must presumably begin where we are.

We must begin where we are. The problems which arise when theology is wedded too closely and exclusively to particular interpretations of the methods of natural scientists are obvious. But similar problems occur in essays in theology and psychology, theology and sociology, anthropology and so on. The answer clearly cannot be found in retreating to some form of traditional dogmatics entirely divorced from other disciplines. Provided that we are able to reflect critically on our own preferences, it must be possible to make progress through making mistakes. All creation is God's creation, and we must seek to understand all human activity in relation to his love in creation and redemption. It may be noticed that the inability of a theoretical framework to meet our need for a general theory need not prevent us from benefiting from its author's proposals on specific issues. This will be evident from our discussion of Pannenberg's Christology. In the nature of the case, too, one of the most important functions of general theories is to give clues to the nature of critical rationality, precisely in the ways in which they break down, and so stimulate the development of modified or conflicting accounts.

Notes to Chapter 5

1 T. W. L. Adorno, *Negative Dialektik* (Suhykamp Verlag, Frankfurt, 1966).
2 Pannenberg, *Theology and the philosophy of science* (DLT, London, 1976).
3 A. Stork, in VF, 1975.
4 T. F. Torrance, *Theological Science* (OUP, 1969). cf. *God and Rationality* (OUP, 1971), *Space, Time and Incarnation* (OUP, 1969), *Space, Time and Resurrection* (Handsel Press, Edinburgh, 1976), *Theology in Reconstruction* (SCM Press, London, 1965). cf. M. Hesse, *The Structure of Scientific Inference* (Macmillan, London, 1974), P. Achinstein and S. Barker (ed.), *The Legacy of Logical Positivism* (Baltimore, 1969), L. Lakatos and A. Musgrave (ed.), *Criticism and the Growth of Knowledge* (Cambridge, 1970). cf. too A. Naess, *The Pluralist and Possibilist Aspects of the Scientific Enterprise* (Oslo, 1972). Naess 30 'In short, what we identify as the phenomena observed depends on our theory, or rather metatheory, of the process of observation'. cf. Quine's famous dictum, 'Any statement can be held true come what may, if we make drastic enough adjustments elsewhere in the system'. Also K. O. Apel, *Analytical Philosophy of Language and the Geisteswissenschaften* (Dordrecht, 1967), and I. Leclerc, *The Nature of Physical Existence* (London, 1972), on Experience cf. J. M. Hinton, op. cit. and J. E. Smith, *The Analogy of Experience*. cf. 'Gödel's theorem is a red herring', I. J. Good in B. J. Phil. Sc., 1968, 357f. Also, on the complex interactions of disposition and evidence in meaning, cf. M. Capek, *The Philosophical Importance of Contemporary Physics* (Princeton, N.J., 1961), and *The Concepts of Space and Time* (Dordrecht, 1976). On the hermeneutical enterprise cf. Gadamer, *Truth and Method* (Sheen & Ward, London, 1975), R. E. Palmer, *Hermeneutics* (Evanston, Ill., 1972).
5 To speak of 'the Jesus of history who has haunted and baffled so many modern historians, for he insists on being understood as true historical event that will not submit to historical criteria we already have at our disposal but will yield his secret to those who are open and ready to consider him in his own majestic self-presentation and self-interpretation' seems to me to be highly obscure.

Chapter 6

God's Love and the Basic Structures of Theology

1

In the face of these severe difficulties, what conclusions may be drawn about the nature of the theological enterprise?[1]

In much recent theology it often seems that frustration with our inability to speak of the presence of the living God, of the grace of God in human life now, leads to the evacuation of the promise into the unverifiable security of the future, a sort of intellectual equivalent of pie in the sky . . . ! What of the *Christus praesens*, the living presence of Christ now in his word and in his salvation, Christ together with all his benefits?

We have seen difficulties too in the theology of the *Word*. If to its credit it reminded us of the initatitive of God in his relations with man, of the factor of God's sheer, unmerited grace, yet it raised questions. If there is no knowledge of God except through the Word in Christ, how can we ever find reasonable grounds for accepting God's invitation in Christ? And we must find these if faith is to be more than an irrational leap in the dark, a mindless obedience to a compelling and mysterious summons. How are we to relate philosophy to theology, Christianity to other religions? If theology is a completely autonomous science, how are we to account for the differences among Christian theologies, and how are we to choose between them? How are we to distinguish between truth and illusion? Can a theology of the word alone do justice to all that the humanity of God in Christ implies? On the one hand perhaps we cannot do without a theology of the word of God, but on the other, we have to avoid the danger of 'verbalization' of the gospel, to which Pannenberg and others have rightly drawn attention.

Part of the problem of the dehumanizing element of an authoritarian word can be tackled by correlation of *word* and *faith*. *Faith* is always trust in things partially unseen. We trust because we know the love of God in Christ, but we do not have the complete knowledge of God for which we await at the end of time. Faith enables us to trust our life to God and his gospel, but it is not a self-evident possibility. We retain cognitive freedom. The gospel is invitation rather than inevitability for us. But at the same time, the openness of faith can become the source of trouble. Anything and everything in life can be brought under the heading of faith. Any kind of relation involving uncertainty or expectation can be seen as a ground of faith. Faith can become so comprehensive that it loses its precise meaning, and so the concept becomes self defeating.

To be effective, the analysis of *faith* has to be tied closely to certain other elements of the Christian tradition, the importance of events in the past, and the experience of the Christian tradition and the believer today within this tradition, to talk of *God*, as the source of faith.

Similar points can be made in respect of hope and of history. These have important but limited roles to play. Certainly these will not in themselves solve the problems of faith and revelation in this century. Probably the same may be said of humanity, the secular, and all the other catchwords of recent theology.

We cannot go back to the certain ties and ontological assurances of the Early Church and the Reformation. The given – is complex.[2] And yet it is not enough to cry complex, and decry all attempts at constructive reconstruction. The motor mechanic can take a car to pieces, the psychiatrist can analyse or even take personality to pieces. But human life needs things to be put together again, if they are to be of use. Theology too should help faith to understand, and so come to a deeper faith. Granted that we may not make faith an epistemological principle. Yet the sphere of worship and commitment will and should affect the way we think about God. The experience of the presence of God in worship, in word and sacrament, should certainly 'make a difference' to the way in which we view God and the world. Understood in this way, revelation and word in worship have a role to play after all.

The problem of excessive preoccupation with preliminary questions can be seen in recent discussion of revelation.[3] It has been suggested that the word 'revelation' should be completely replaced by 'salvation'. 'Revelation', it may be argued, is not a central category in scripture, revelation as propositional is difficult to reconcile with the many different theologies among Christians, I-Thou encounter cannot be proved in the case of God in the same way as in human meetings, and revelation cannot be justified by philosophical analysis or by biblical or Christian tradition. In any case, revelation cannot be discussed in isolation from salvation – a good point. Yet it is difficult to see how we can enjoy the gift of salvation without some sort of awareness of the fact that God has acted in the interest of human welfare – which tells us something of the nature of the giver of salvation: this is the kind of knowledge. 'The myth of the divine love in Christ creates a possibility of commitment to forms of agape not open to those who do not or cannot accept it.' But if no truth condition can be satisfied, if the 'myth' is in no sense descriptive of a divine reality, then it is doubtful if the commitment distinctive of faith will take place. God becomes a postulate who is ultimately unnecessary. Without something of that which is traditionally spoken of in terms of revelation of knowledge together with salvation, it seems that an adequate explanation of faith is not possible.

2

The love of God can be seen as itself providing knowledge of God, provided that we relate salvation to the events in history and in word narrated in the Bible, and taken up in faith's response in the worshipping and loving tradition of the Church. This then has to be analysed to avoid the imprecision which has bedevilled so many analyses of love in the past. Such an approach may underline areas inadequately explored under the rubrics of faith and hope, history and revelation. But all the time we have to bear in mind that the 'love' model too has to be qualified and precisely related to particular historical and theological data. Love can be a monster, an instrument of power, of cruelty, or possessiveness, of hatred and destruction. The love of God is important, but love can be the excuse both for failure to attempt to explain what it is to speak of the action of God in Christ among men, and also for failure to grapple with concrete problems of what loving involves. Faith is important, but must not be an excuse for relating all human experience of openness to God without further analysis. Hope is important, but must not mean the abandoning of the claim that God in Christ is present here and now, and that the hope of the future is based firmly on the past and the present. Word and revelation are important, but involve also salvation and history. History is important, but we must take seriously the charge that anyone who says 'history' has nothing to say to the present. The presence of God in Christ now is important, but the nature of the given in theology is complex. Complexity is important, but does not mean that we can avoid demands for truth claims on the one hand, and on the other hand the insistence that faith is not to be confused with complete knowledge. There are things which the Christian simply does not know, at least in the way that he knows of everything within the created world. Humanity is important, but some of the most eloquent analyses of humanity never mention the word: they only describe detailed situations, e.g. Solzhenitzyn's *The First Circle*. The humanity of God in Christ makes possible a new humanity. But it is neither possible nor desirable to attempt to explain divinity purely in terms of humanity. The transcendental reference must be carefully and painfully maintained. Humanity is too weak and too limited to explain divinity exhaustively (Lutheran doctrines on the kenosis of God in Christ notwithstanding). Salvation and revelation must be distinguished but not separated, and given full weight. Faith is lived out in the Church, but also in the world. The Church is not only a part of the world, for Christians are in one sense citizens of another realm. But at the same time the function of the Church here and now is to serve the world, both through worship, prayer and teaching, and also through assistance in humanizing the world. Humanization of the world also includes the conversion of the world to Christ. In this, the gospel is distinguished but not isolated from all other spheres of human welfare. In fundamental theology, problems of the analysis of language and of metaphysics are unavoidable, but these must also be combined with insight into the historicality of all understanding and indeed of all our living. To this extent theology should be electic, for it is concerned with all the achievements and questions of human reason, and not simply with local interests. If understanding the atom is child's play compared with understanding child's play, then, complex as humanity is, God is even more complex, and the theoretical explanation of relations between God and his creation is highly complex: theology IS difficult. But for the child to play is natural, and understanding his play is for him no problem. So faith, it may be said, comes naturally to the children of God as they take up through grace his invitation to salvation in Christ. But as they begin to reflect critically upon this, then they are involved in complex reflection which at the same time raises questions of faith itself. And so is set up the reciprocal relation between faith and question.

3

The focal point of all discussion in Christian theology is the Gospel of God as this is appropriated by men, at the present time and in the light of the tradition of faith in God in Israel, in the New Testament and in the Church.

The Gospel message, spelled out in different ways in different parts of the New Testament and in the development of Christian tradition, involves certain specific common affirmations and claims. These claims concern the importance for men of certain historical events before the coming of Jesus, during his life and afterwards. In these events, historical data of different kinds, including in different degrees the element of interpretation, is present.

These historical events impinge upon the nature and destiny of man, according to the Gospel message. They also involve claims about the relation of the way things are in the physical universe, and inhuman society, in relation to each other and to God, who is claimed to be the creator and sustainer of the universe. To this extent the New Testament reflects and in part endorses the ancient world's concern with theism.

The centre of the Gospel is an invitation to enter into a relationship with God, a relationship which involves trust in God who fulfils the destiny of men. When a man enters into this relationship in faith, in trusting himself to God, within the experience of the worshipping community of those who live as committed to God in their lives, then he becomes aware of the imperfection and inadequacy of life without God.

This does not, however, turn his faith into knowledge, for he still lives in the condition of human finitude, even in the presence of Christ which is recognized in the worship of the community, and unrecognized in the world. Indeed, his own imperfections become more obvious in the light of the presence of the crucified Christ.

At the same time, reflection upon faith is open to all the

methods which other human reflection employs. Historical claims are open to the usual types of historical enquiry. Metaphysical claims about the nature of God involve by definition an element of mystery, where the bounds of sense are crossed in discussion of the transcendent; but even here the assertions are open to the strictest scrutiny.

Claims about the nature and destiny of man are open to examination in terms of philosophical and social anthropology, psychology, and indeed all the human and natural sciences.

Even the language in which the claims are made is open to examination in terms of every available methods of enquiry. The claim that God has chosen human language to make known his purpose of fulfilment to his creation is not verifiable exhaustively, for this would remove the element of the grace of God and the cognitive freedom of men. But it must at least be verifiable to the extent that it becomes a reasonable option for the man who chooses faith. These events are of a particular character and make a particular impact upon him. So for example he is constantly made aware of his dependence upon others from birth, in family and in social contexts. He needs food, which can only be obtained at least in childhood with the help of others, and soon he needs personal relationships of different kinds. He expresses himself in play, in different ways, including such sophisticated types of play as art, music and religion. Sometimes he finds himself helping others: sometimes others help him, but they cannot rely on him *always* being helpful, nor he on them. His understanding is limited. He does not know the answers to all his questions. He knows more than some people know but some know more than he does. The kind of people he associated with, and the geographical environment, help to shape the way in which his society lived, the rules and conventions by which it keeps together. All of these things may be thought of as mere truisms.[4] Experience of living in a social context leads some men at least to seek for ultimate meaning in life, to search in philosophical anthropologies for the transcendent: this is on the whole recognized to be unfulfilled. The search is expressed in the appreciation of art, music, beauty and so on. Against this understanding of fulfilment is to be placed all the evil, suffering, limitation and deficiency in the world at large and in the hearts of men. This means that only a suffering God can help: it is through the history of the suffering and pain of God in Jesus Christ that religion can satisfy the need of men for fulfilment, for meaning in life. But this history must be more than the appearance of a beautiful idea. If it is to be acceptable, its truth has to be checked out in relation to historical events, like other events in history. Such a history of the compassion of God must also be verifiable on a wider plane if it is to be comprehensible as the love of God. It must be seen also to be at least not completely contradictory to our knowledge of the way things are in the universe. The historical data of the Christ event must be related too to my experience of the world now. Does Christian faith help me to understand the course of my life, and to live my life in accordance with its claims? If faith in God reflected upon in relation to the rest of human knowledge and experience, leads some men at least to a deeper understanding of this, and so to a deeper faith, then it may be claimed to be not simply an irrational choice but the way, the truth and the life. There are many people today who would answer this question in the affirmative, and who would put their answer down to the grace of God himself. If this is so, then faith and revelation, reason and grace are not ultimately incompatible. I suggest that Christian faith must be comprehensible in terms of, not falsified by, all that men can discover about the physical universe. This I think is as far as the demand for this particular truth condition can go. It is not possible to verify the existence, action or presence of God in the physical universe in the way in which we can verify the presence of physical objects. For the God of Christian faith is not himself part of his creation, not an object in the world of objects, but rather the supreme subject. Only in his secondary objectivity as it were in the incarnation does he enter into his creation completely.

The Christian claim is that the universe is the creation of God and so God is the origin and key to the truth of the way things are in the physical universe. Christ is the way, the truth and the life. One of the key functions of the Holy Spirit is to lead us into all truth. This means that we seek to explore the meaning of the life of man in the universe in all its different modes, believing that as we explore each area of discourse, trying to relate human experience and theory to talk about God and his Gospel, this will lead us into a deeper understanding of God and his ways with men. There is potentially no area of discourse which cannot enable us to deepen our understanding of God and man, provided that we continue to centre this discourse upon the Gospel as expressed in the Bible, the traditions and the living presence of God in worship and in discipleship. As our understanding deepens, the way in which we see the Gospel will change in perspective. This is, as it were, the complexity of the given, but at the same time the New Testament message of God's love itself will remain, through prayer and the grace of God, the centre, even while the perspective changes. Where the position of God's love in Christ becomes peripheral, then faith becomes less than faithful and our vision can only be distorted, our love grows weaker and our openness to the love of God less complete. *Fecisti enim nos ad te Deus, et cor nostrum est inquietum donec requiescat in te*. And that after all, is what theology is about!

4

I want to return now to the perennially thorny problem of the relation of the subjective to the objective in theology, and to theology as the dialectically related search for deeper knowledge of God and of man, *Dei cognitio et hominis*.

Experience is an important element in theological construction. Experience has been especially prominent of course in modern theology since it was used by Schleiermacher as the key element in his brilliant theological reconstruction. In turn it became suspect under the influence of Karl Barth.

There is a vast assortment of states of affairs which can be, and often are, described by the general term experiences.[5] Sometimes all theology is summed up as based on experience. But it seems to me that this generalization is open to similar objections to those which are found in looking at tradition, as the epitomized experience of the community. Why should we accept traditions or experiences as authoritative, how do we make selections between conflicting experiences or traditions, and how do we guard against the manifold problems and indeed probabilities of self-deception? At the same time, answers may be found to these questions, and we must not simply write off an important source of theological reflection simply because it has its dangers. Most worthwhile intellectual activities involve the risk of being mistaken, but may still be of value despite the mistakes.

A good illustration of this approach can be seen in the strong appeal to experience characteristic of the recent report of the Archbishops' Doctrine Commission.[6] It may well be that there has been some uncertainty here about the relation of cultural relativism to cultural relativity. But at least the essays are infinitely better than resort to what McLeod Campbell described long ago as the self-congratulations of a blind orthodoxy.

The great philosophers have always recognized that the basic problems of philosophy are just intrinsically difficult, and are not to be finally resolved by the general application of any particular logical, epistemological or metaphysical system. *A fortiori*, the same applies to the intellectual foundations of theology. General appeals to revelation, experience, dynamic activity, history and the like may be

imaginative and stimulating, may assist in focusing attention, but will not in themselves 'solve' anything.

Looking again at the area of experience, human auto-
nomy and subjectivity, one can produce some propositions
which will command fairly universal agreement. All human
apprehension come to us through experience, i.e. it is interpreted in being appropriated by us, within a particular
cultural framework, even if this framework is itself divisible
into a number of overlapping frameworks. But though in
talking of God we may, though logically we need not, start
from experience, we may discover new things about God
which lead us to revise our views in the light of this experience (so with food, people, books, etc). we can recognize,
discover, invent and interpret, and these processes are by no
means mutually exclusive. Our beliefs about the nature of
theological truth need not be strictly limited by the account
we are able to give about how we come to know this truth,
nor need it correspond precisely to the structure of our
theories of knowledge.

We may come to believe that certain states of affairs are
the case concerning God which do not derive from our direct
experience (as in other fields, like human relations, microbiology, historical research, astrophysics, etc.). If our starting point is to be human experience we must endeavour not
to continue and end with human experience alone. This applies equally to other points such as The Word, and history.
The starting point is optional. What counts is whether the
completed construction offers an adequate account of central structuring elements in the particular area of theology
under consideration.

5

I believe that as a matter of fact there is not, and in principle there never can be, one preferred and privileged start-

ing point in theology. People who believe they have such a preferred position tend in practice often to produce an exclusive theology, seeing themselves as the guardians of a pure and sacred tradition, and all others as somehow intellectually and often morally deficient. They often combine this with insistence upon openness, and freedom, but this is a strictly circumscribed freedom. True freedom involves the recognition that others have valid perspectives, and that one is engaged in making a contribution together with others. True freedom must involve the freedom to disagree with as well as to agree with others, but on a basis of mutual respect, a willingness to listen without prior acceptability conditions. It is a curious irony that theologians who have often insisted most strongly on the impropriety of imposing limits on the sovereign freedom of God have themselves been most intransigent in refusing to enter into genuine dialogue with their fellow Christians, not to speak of the rest of God's reconciled humanity.

Pluralism in theology has come to stay. This is a permanent legacy of the European Enlightenment and of the development of modern society. This does not mean, however, 'blessed are the empty-minded'. Though revelation never comes 'neat', if it is devoid of specific propositional content it is meaningless and inconsequential. Despite the personal quality of God's relationship with mankind, I-Thou relationships can always be articulated with the aid of a considerable number of I-It propositions, which need in no way detract from the personal nature of truth. Theology is concerned not simply with the interpretation of literature about life, nor with the interpretation of personal reactions. It is concerned with states of affairs in the universe recognized as God's creation as well as a physical environment. This becomes particularly acute in facing the problem of evil, as we have seen. God's relation to the events in Auschwitz in our time, is neither literary nor contemplative nor indeed simply pragmatic and empirical. It is that of the creator who through the spirit of Christ has finally bound himself to his creation as the anticipation of an ultimate reality. Put in a technical phrase, faith in this divine reality can afford neither to be concealed pragmatism nor romantic fideism. As faith it is an enterprise *in via* rather than *in patria*. But it is faith in an external transcendent referent, on the basis of the cumulative case with which this whole study has been concerned, rather than faith in faith. The non-objectifiability of God, stressed in theology since Kant, has to be understood as the hiddenness of God through the cross rather than an epistemological maxim working with a one-to-one correspondence between the hidden God and all aspects of our talk of God. Such hiddenness leads to mystification rather than mystery.

In recent work there has been much preoccupation with theology as story, sometimes over against a theology of experience. The story of salvation needs simply to be told in order to have a self-authenticating, but not necessarily authoritarian, effect. I don't myself think that all that matters is to tell the story. The Bible, as we suggested, contains not a story but a library of salvation, with different and often conflicting genres of story represented. If we are to speak of self-disclosure in story, we must include in principle the areas of interpretation on the one hand and the basic metaphysical ideas of the nature of the divine agent and his activity in creation on the other. The story is then useful as a guide to further reflection rather than as itself the goal of reflection. The story has been seen as a recital of the acts of God. But we have already seen that the act of God for one person need not be the act of God for another. There may be many different sorts and levels of acts of God. Acts of God are always interpreted, but not all interpretations are equally true. Some interpretations can be shown, by listing advantages and objections, to be more central to Christian faith than others. In practice we reject the more eccentric fringe interpretations on precisely these grounds.

6

In speaking of the adequacy or otherwise of accounts of theology we refer to central and structuring elements – on this account based on God's love in Christ. These are related to ordinary criteria for interpreting everyday experience, but are not identical with it. For despite the fact that our world is God's world, it is I think inaccurate to characterize religious experience as ordinary experience. On the contrary, it is illuminating precisely in happening 'against the odds' in unfolding often briefly a new dimension in existence. Neither Christology, nor history nor experience nor talk of encounter will suffice for a sufficient account of the theological dimensions of this existence. All may be helpful however in leading us to widen the horizon of our understanding to include imaginative reflection on the hidden transcendence of God.

If we speak of the nature of authority in theology, then it is clear that this can only be the authority of God. Neither the Bible, the tradition, the Church or the current assumptions of society, academic or otherwise, can provide final authority, though they may provide indispensable illumination. Because of this final openness to God's transcendence, theology may be though it has not always been, the final protector of the individual human conscience as responsible ultimately only to God the creator, and as sustained ultimately and indestructibly by God the redeemer. Understood in this way, the love of God through the cross and resurrection of Christ and mediated through the Spirit is the ultimate basis of human freedom, intellectual, social and political. The love of God is at the same time a judgement on all human limitation of freedom where that limitation hinders rather than assists the full articulation of the divine love in creation for all mankind. Christian freedom as the freedom of love, is not about the Church, its intellectual and cultural purity, well being, etc, but about the whole of humanity, however difficult to speak of this highly multiplex body may be, and about the Church as the servant of God, and man for God and man.

Notes to Chapter 6

1 For discussion of the issues involved in any comprehensive fundamental theology cf. e.g. D. Tracy, *Blessed Rage for Order,* (Seabury Press, N.Y. 1975) and H. Peukert, *Wissenschafts-theorie, Handlungstheorie, Fundamentale Theologie,* (Patmos, Düsseldorf, 1976).

2 cf. J. McIntyre, *The Shape of Christology* (SCM Press, London, 1966).

3 cf. G. Downing, *Has Christianity a Revelation?* (SCM Press, London, 1964).

4 On humanity and philosophical anthropology, cf. R. S. Downie, *Roles and Values* (Methuen, London, 1971).

5 cf. J. M. Hinton, *Experiences*, op. cit.

6 *Christian Believing* (SPCK, London, 1976). cf. my comments in 'Systematic Theology, 1971-76', *Epworth Review*, Jan. 1977, 110ff.

Chapter 7

The Love of God
the Creator

1

There are innumerable ways of talking about deity. The many different concepts of God involved can then be combined in various ways with other areas of religious traditions in order to define them more closely. The justification for particular choices or combinations will lie in the ways in which they are used. In concentrating upon God's love I can claim that such an understanding of God belongs to the classical Christian tradition of faith, life and worship. The resonance which such an interpretation of the biblical narratives has found in Christian faith is itself part of the grounds, though not the only ground, for regarding it as central. At the same time the inevitable complexity of human talk of the transcendent God always carries with it the twin and opposite temptations of concluding that all is equally uncertain or finding some miraculous device to cut the Gordian knot.

It is obvious that all Christian talk of God is intimately related to the events concerning Jesus of Nazareth, whether we are speaking of God as creator or as redeemer. But nothing is to be gained by swallowing up the doctrine of creation into Christology. Many religions are concerned importantly with God as creator, and here Christianity is no exception. In speaking of the love of God the creator I want to work out further implication of the clue to God as love which is given in the events concerning Jesus, love as the self-giving, self-affirming nature of God. This narrative clue may be summed up as follows.

God's love involves caring, caring continuously for the whole created order. It is to God that the universe owes its continuing existence. We observe, as Schleiermacher pointed out in a famous passage, that the world is preserved in creation. In the Christian community we are aware in the response of faith that it is God who is the author and sustainer of this creation. How can this be, and how are we to understand God as our creator?

2

The God who loves is a personal God. To say this is at once to make a decisive affirmation and to raise a number of insoluble problems. There are concepts of deity which are impersonal and these have sometimes provided valuable correctives to narrowly personal interpretations of God. As has often been pointed out, people who make 'personal' remarks are often being at their most objectionable, and in any case the creator of the universe is more than a person in the sense of an individual human being. But though God may be personal in ways different from human ways of being personal, he is not, for the biblical narratives and for the faith of most Christians, less than personal. In particular, the biblical testimony to the nature of God as involved in human experience in the events concerning Jesus will lead one to recommend personal and disrecommend impersonal conceptions of God.

Though it is extremely difficult to produce exhaustive philosophical definitions of what it is to be a person, it is possible to make some significant distinctions. We can all distinguish between persons and other beings, and we can distinguish treating persons as persons from treating them as objects. We make distinctions, splitting up the notion of person, in Strawson's well-known phrase a 'logically primitive' concept, into further notions: self, consciousness, action, motivation, willing, believing and so on.[1] Similar distinctions are made in speaking of God. It is true that talk of the transcendent is a great deal more complex than talk of human persons, but we must try to understand what we mean in speaking of God as a transcendent self, acting in the world, having feelings, willing. It may be objected at once that we cannot know how God feels. But as in the knowledge of the feelings of other persons, we can have such knowledge as is disclosed by the other to us. In the case of God, this raises again the questions of how we in our finitude can understand God, revelation or not. In an age of increasing secularization, at no time has the need for carefully stated rational grounds – which is not of course the same as rationalism – been more pressing.

Let me emphasize again exactly what I am asserting. I wish to maintain that the Christian God is love, radically and utlimately love, love alone, love in some respects hidden in ultimate mystery and in others revealed through the tradition of the biblical narratives within the Judaeo-Christian communities. There is no descriptive term of a higher order of importance than love in respect to the Christian God. As such he is loving creator, and is personal in himself and in relation to his created order.

3

God is personal, and he is also the creator of the universe. However we may view the processes of physical creation – and cosmology is one of the most rapidly developing of the theoretical sciences – Christian faith believes that God is the ultimate source of all being, and that he continues to sustain, care for, direct and have ultimate responsibility for the whole created order. Faith affirms that God knows all the needs of his creatures, feels for them in their various situations and acts on behalf of all of them, bringing comfort and directing them towards the fulfilment of his purpose for them. Viewed from any standpoint, but especially from the awareness of the minuteness of the earth in cosmological perspective and the biochemically contingent nature of humanity in the perspective of the live sciences, the claims of Christian faith are indeed on a vast scale.[2]

One way of facing the difficulties, popular at least since the European Enlightenment is to suggest first that such claims are no longer tenable, and second that they are highly anthropomorphic, projecting human desires for security and authority, and so are in fact un-Christian. This has led to new definitions of the essence of Christianity, and new concepts of God to match. It is easy to dismiss all revisions of traditional theology as reductionism. But the challenge posed to theology by the Enlightenment is indeed enormous, and in my view has yet to be successfully overcome. Many of the so called 'high' doctrines of faith with which theologians have answered criticism have been excessively anthropomorphic and intellectually untenable. Neither drastic revision nor embattled reiteration appear to be appropriate.

It has been and continues to be of central importance for Christians to affirm that God is able to feel for his creatures, and to understand intimately their feelings. He must be able simultaneously to suffer with those who are in distress and to rejoice with those who rejoice. A God who cannot do this is scarcely worthy of disbelief not to speak of belief. That God is involved with creation in this way we have affirmed from the focal point of his engagement in the events concerning Jesus. It is hard to say that God's loving care for mankind is to be deduced from observation of the world of nature. For some this appears to be so, but for others it does not. Evil and suffering, chance and necessity raise massive problems about providence, and prevent us from reading off the benevolent will of God from observation of the world, in the manner made famous by William Paley.

We have said already that we cannot deduce a structure for the transcendent referent, God from the concept of love itself. We cannot claim that it is logically necessary in a doctrine of God that his concern should extend to feeling for his creation. Even in Christianity, especially in deist traditions, the notion that God is intimately involved in relationship with his creatures is eliminated, and many people have found and find such reconstructions helpful. My suggestion is that such reconstructions amount to less than a true account of Christian faith. This does not mean, as is sometimes suggested by people who hold quasi-deist positions, that the only alternative is a position in which God becomes a sort of instantly available personal servant of each individual. The freedom of the transcendent God excludes both deism and exaggerated individualism alike.

4

In considering criteria for talk of the Christian God we have mentioned experience. Experience of God is reflected in the Bible, the tradition and contemporary belief. Experience may be interpreted in different ways, theistically or non-theistically, religiously or not. The interpretation occurs in relation to other considerations often of a rational and historical nature. People have been able to believe in the love of God when their experience has been predominantly of the absence rather than the presence of God, at times of appalling desolation, in concentration camp situations and the like. This is in part at least because the grounds for faith include remembrance of God's promise and goodness in the past, and hope in God for the future, as well as present experience. Experience is particularly open to cultural conditioning, and is liable to be more or less intense at different times and in different situations. Experience counts, but as the cumulative effect of occasions related to oneself and others, rather than as a continuous touchstone of presence or absence.

When we think of confirmation from experience of God's loving care for all his creatures, then the notion of the sense of presence of God comes to mind. This notion has a long history in theology. It is clear that an understanding of the Christian God which relied solely on talk of God's mighty acts in the past and on hope of his coming in the future without present would be a sterile faith. Such an understanding of faith could be said to evacuate the problems of the present into the twin havens of the security of the past and the unverifiable future. Anyone who has read John Baillie's *The Sense of the Presence of God* will know that notions of presence cannot be dismissed as simply the legacy of nineteenth-century European idealism in modern theology, even though that tradition may have been a starting point for much reflection on presence. At the same time, presence is a complex concept which has advantages and disadvantages in speaking of the transcendent. It may be that nearness, not in the sense of 'and so actually absent', but as more intimately present than any other experience and yet not present as one human being may be to another, is a better term. Some such understanding of nearness is articulated, in a quite different framework, in Aquinas' understanding of the interaction of grace and nature in primary and secondary causality.[3]

A very different avenue towards the more adequate articulation of God's engagement with his creation has been developed in process thought. Process theologians have noted the reliance of much traditional theology on an Aristotelian doctrine of the impassibility of God, hard to reconcile with any notion of God's involvement with the world. Much of the unsympathetic criticism which has been levelled at this movement stems from adherence to the same tradition of divine impassibility. We have already noted in

D. D. Williams' work a mature and original use of process thought along these lines. But though traditions of impassibility have posed insuperable problems for the articulation of an adequate account of God's concern, the notion of the world in God suggested in pantheism may lead to incoherence in the doctrine of God. The solution, however, can scarcely take the form of a return from the new inadequacies to the old.[4]

A further approach to the articulation of God's concern for the created order is by renewed concentration on the relations of creation and redemption. God's feeling for us is understood through God's involvement in death through the death and resurrection of Jesus. This leads to the affirmation of God's nature as essentially involving loving relationship in the trinitarian structure of God's person. We have already spoken of Barth's understanding of God as the triune God. Here the strength lies in the exposition and affirmation rather than in the explanation of the conceptual difficulties.

5

In order to reach a fuller understanding of the love of God the creator we must consider the implications of the attribution of being and action to God. What sort of a being is God, if he is a being, and how does he act towards us? It has sometimes been fashionable in modern theology to abandon talk of being in favour of action. But any such division between functional and ontological categories and the like ultimately breaks down. We cannot have action without an agent, agent without being. This does not of course imply the use of any particular account of the nature of being. One of the best Christian accounts of the being of God, classical yet in its own way revolutionary, was given by St Thomas Aquinas. God for Thomas is the supremely existent one, the prime mover (thought not, above all, in his essential nature love). Like Augustine, Luther and Barth, he is concerned to take account from the beginning of the hiddenness of God. 'We cannot consider concerning God how he is, but rather how he is not' (ST.1q2.a.3). He is pure actuality, without unrealized potentiality. In thinking and willing he realizes a goal which is related to his own nature, existing in the world in goodness and love. He could bring the world to perfection however he wishes, but in fact has chosen to operate supremely through the incarnation.

The being (esse) of God does not refer simply to that which is, but stresses the role of action in being. Esse is the act by which a thing is. There is a close relation between the pairs essence and existence and potentiality and actuality, which derives from Thomas' doctrine of creation. The act of existence comes to the created order from outside. The existence of created things depends on their esse which is God. Only in God are esse and existence identical. God is pure actuality, because his nature is the act of pure existence. Created beings, on the other hand, participate in esse as something given by God, without existing in the same way as God does. So in the creature, though not in God, there is a real distinction between esse and essentia.

The kind of existence the world has is shaped by its essential being, its perfect actualization, which remains for the moment with God. To exist then is not a static thing but an act of being, whose perfection remains with God. Only God is self-existence, i.e. essence is supremely realized existence. Such an existence is developed further in Thomas' understanding of the trinity. As the trinitarian God, God is not remote from the world, but acts immediately and intimately in all things, being constantly present in his creation in a number of different ways, through his essence in sustaining the created order through grace in all humanity and in a special way through Christ.[5]

6

I would like to develop discussion of God's being from the

account given of the love of God in Eberhard Jüngel's major work *God as the Secret of the World*. There is considerable emphasis on God as love in Jüngel's work.[6] He can speak of love as the basic structure of theology, and of the identity of God and love. 'God has defined himself as love on the cross.' In love we are changed from those who have into those who are. Then we can say that God is love. As love, he is the secret of the world. We may feel that Jüngel's contrast between being and having, which he takes up from Erich Fromm, is something of an over-simplification. But the proposal is everywhere creative and ingenious.

'The concept of God follows from Christian faith itself', i.e. we start from revelation rather than natural theology. God is love. There is a basic analogy for talk of God, but it is, following Barth, an *analogia fidei*. The key to the analogy is Jesus, who is himself God's parable. He constitutes the humanity of God. God's humanity, which is the means of our understanding him, is unfolded to our understanding in the telling of the story of Jesus. God is the *secret* of the world in that he comes through Jesus, and in no other way, though an open secret. The appropriate human response to God's coming is in the fruits of faith, hope and love.

This is clearly writing from within the Christian tradition to those outside. The problems remain however of how one comes from an 'outside' view to an inside view. Little explanation is forthcoming. Since we all live, and as Christians ought to live, in a number of overlapping intellectual communities, and share the perplexities of understanding felt by those 'outside', clearly more needs to be done. *The* major cruxes are taken for granted. We have already noted the difficulty of the Christological answer without further reference. It may be necessary, vital and central; but it is not sufficient, even if our further discussion is inevitably incomplete. How can we see the manifestation of *God* in Jesus without any prior notion of what God might be like? How is this concept of God to be related to God in other religions, if at all, etc?

We have here, pursued resolutely, an understanding of a
theology of the cross. 'The crucified one is *the* criterion for a
possible concept of God.' From the point of view of the
world, God is in no sense 'necessary', and so all natural
theology based on demonstrating such a necessity is futile. It
was the merit of Hegel to understand God's participation in
death on the cross as the basis of a philosophical possibility
for talk of the Christian God. God can be thought of, not
from the world as a starting point but from the Word.
Neither negative nor positive theology can be justified, but
only theology arising from Jesus as *the* parable of God.
Because God exists and makes himself known in different
self-differentiation through Jesus, the Trinity is the appropriate expression of God as a living God, involved in
creation and salvation.

Here is a thoughtful answer to the question of the nature
of the Christian God. It cannot be a complete answer, however, as long as it does not engage explicitly with the innumerable further questions which men raise. How does this
trinitarian, cross-centred concept of God related to men's
questions about the nature of human existence in society,
and the nature and purpose of the cosmos? *How* is the word
to be related to history and truth? Jüngel has understood
clearly that the secret of the world, though an open secret, is
mysterious and profound. It is probably, however, rather
more mysterious than even this proposal suggests.

7

Continental theology continues to develop theories of understanding the being of God, and tends to operate with what
we may regard as an undue ontological confidence. Anglo-
Saxon theology, on the other hand, is often more concerned
with the action of God, and tends to operate with undue
epistemological pessimism. We may illustrate this later

situation by looking at the work of the leading and influential American theologian, Gordon Kaufman, especially in his work *God the Problem*. It is perhaps no accident that God here is not a secret but a problem. The central concern is with the uses of religious language, and especially with talk of God as agent. Our understanding of God should be based on our understanding of ourselves as agents. The real God is in principle completely unknown, because God is always beyond our experience and our philosophical concepts. Kaufman's discussion is valuable, but suffers from the telescoping of a number of related but not identical issues.[7]

In speaking of God's action there may be something to be learned from Austin Farrer's adaptation of Aquinas' discussion of primary and secondary causality. But actions and events are not themselves simple entities, and so Aquinas' solutions will scarcely provide more than directions, signposts for understanding rather than explanations. But at least St Thomas did see that it is possible for God, as for people, to act at different times in different ways and occasionally in different ways at the same time.[8]

Kaufman's argument provides an instructive foil to Jüngel's. 'As the Creator or source of all that is, God is not to be identified with any particular finite reality: as the proper object of ultimate loyalty or faith, God is to be distinguished from every proximate or penultimate value or being.' But if absolutely nothing within our experience can be directly identified as that to which the term "God" properly refers, what meaning does or can the word have?' Kaufman faces the challenge of the modern consciousness of the absence of God from the world. He accepts that God as an infinitely transcendent source of being cannot be involved in any 'intervention' in the world. But meaningfulness is related to correspondence with facts in the natural world, therefore God's meaning becomes highly problematic. This solution to the dilemma has been attacked trenchantly by philosophers. The whole of creation is regarded as part of a single master act 'of God', of whom we can continue to speak only in highly metaphorical language.

Kaufman favours talk of God as agent. But we can speak of God as agent only by analogy with ourselves as agents. However, God remains basically unknown, and so we can say nothing of specific examples of God's actions. Process philosophy can resolve this problem by regarding the world as God's body. But this raises more difficulties for Christian faith than it solves (though process concepts can be used with advantage in theology in other directions). God's action is conceived as one master act which is constituted by the whole course of history. The master act may include sub-acts, but these cannot be distinguished with certainty. But acts themselves may be of different sorts, and there are numerous further possible differentiations between certain sorts of acts and certain sorts of events. It has been suggested in further discussion that no amount of experimental evidence can possibly count for or against the suggestion that God acts, and that all we can hope to affirm is that God enters into reciprocity with the world. It seems to me that this is too general and too sceptical: at least we can affirm in faith the specific activity of God in the events concerning Jesus.

It emerges from this discussion both that the basis of talk about God's action is hard to explicate and also that conclusions which he reaches are neither inevitable nor viable in the face of philosophical attack. Talk of God's acts, like all other formulaic phrases, will not in themselves produce new theological proposals. James Barr in particular has shown how the talk of acts of God in the biblical narratives is not always as illuminating as has often been assumed. But given the need for caution, it remains the theologian's task to explore new ways of speaking of God's action as of his being, as long as Christians still want to speak of God as supremely personal. Without such affirmation, Christian faith as a living faith in a living God would not exist.

Theological discussion has suffered from lack of awareness of the complex character of acts and events. Acts need not always be thought of as indivisible individual units, as in some sort of billiard ball model of the atom. The nature of causality is exceedingly hard to explain. Parts of some events influence parts of other events. Events bring about states of affairs, encourage further activities and vice versa. If this is the case for comparatively simple events such as 'John won the game' or 'Mary sang the song', the complexity of such multiplex events as 'the event of the incarnation of God in Jesus Christ' can scarcely be imagined. On the other hand, it should be possible for the theologian to consider the theological issues involved in the Christian affirmation of God's sustaining and directing creativity without attempting to take over tasks which belong to the proper function of professional philosphers.

It can be affirmed, with Jüngel and much traditional talk about God, that God is hidden in the world, that he works through grace, that his activity is not to be 'read off' the external world by measurement. But this activity of the hidden love of God is no less real for being hidden. Because affirmation of his presence is 'against the odds', this need not become an occasion to rule out his activity. His purposes, intentions, responsible activity within the events in the natural world remain as open to the response of faith as they have always been. Somewhat as in our knowledge of other minds, there is much which inevitably we are not in a position to observe. This hiddenness is related to God's nature as self-differentiated through the events concerning Jesus, and through the work of God's spirit. Experimental evidence *does* count for and against God's action.[9] But it does not count exhaustively or conclusively. There is a reciprocity between nature and grace, but such that grace, persuasive but not coercive, is always the creative source of love in the world.

8

To return to our earlier question, how is it that God who is love, acts in particular providence in exercising concern for individuals in their daily lives, yet leaves them that personal freedom which is a basic element of human integrity? He is not seen or felt to act in any empirically measurable manner. What then could count as supporting evidence for such assertions? We are involved here with the understanding of grace, the grace of the loving God. Grace must not be used, as it has often been used, as a substitute for explanation. Introduction of the concept can be at best the beginning of an explanation. Grace can scarcely be an invitation to disregard the hypotheses which cumulatively make up the sum of our scientific knowledge about man's place in the physical universe. It does however suggest that the activities of the transcendent God may not be capable of exhaustive explanation within the acceptability criteria which we quite properly apply in our conceptual framework relating to non-theistic referents. The epistemological problems relating to agency and causality remain a matter of continuing philosophical debate. But we must still attempt to indicate the sort of things which we have in mind when referring to God's action, and offer analogies for understanding this action the better.

Virtually all our talk of God employs analogies of different sorts. If all were analogy, then we could scarcely include an element of knowledge in our account of faith. In the scholastic tradition, though St Thomas was well aware of the limitations of doctrines of analogy others were not. There was once a kind of sociological consensus that when men spoke of the traditional attributes of God, omniscience, omnipotence and the like, they were speaking directly of God. The use of analogy was often misleading. God could be conceived of as a kind of medieval monarch, rather than one whose strength was to be seen, as Luther held, in the weakness of the cross. Today we may still use talk of attributes, not as blueprints of God's nature but as imaginative pointers to God, images of a parabolic character pointing to implications of God's love. For us the consolations open to some of the medievals, if not to Thomas, are barred. Transcendent entities often appear to dissolve on closer in-spection into bundles of physical data interpreted by the un-known mechanisms explored in the physiology of the brain. But in that respect at least, talk of God and of things in this world remains almost equally mysterious.

There are further considerations involved in response to the action of a transcendent being. Philosophers have dis-cussed the analogy of the stranger whom we may learn to trust, even when his actions are on occasion hard to inter-pret.[10] The complex nature of relationships in human society often makes it hard to fathom the reasons and justification for men's acts. We cannot perhaps demand instant intelligibility of God either, especially if we believe that he is not, as the loving God, one who forces his will on his creation, but rather invites our participation by leading us on from within our world. This is the truth in the notions of cognitive freedom and epistemic distance. God is content to stand at the door and wait.

We have noted that analogies from individuals are not enough in speaking of God's love. Western thought has, as is often realized, suffered from too exclusive a concept of the value of the individual. Individual freedom is absolutely essential to humanity seen in the light of God's love. Love for all implies a power able to be concerned with all, not diminished by the presence of evil.

God conceived of as a polite but impotent conversation partner with the educated intellectual may satisfy the academic, but is scarcely the Lord of heaven and earth. It is perhaps natural that God in an ancient university should be conceived somewhat on the model of a college tutor, whose authority is highly elusive, who is there when you want him, not there when you don't, who is non-directive, generally benevolent yet not directly involved in the affairs of others, interested in the world of affairs yet not involved in it. It is natural that God among oppressed nations of the Third World should often be seen as the strong leader who will raise up the oppressed against their tormentors in political or military revolution. Both concepts take a highly simplified view of the human situation, whether in college or commune. Presumably we ought not to press God into shapes that are unfitted even for the understanding of men.[11]

How God is and how he acts remains mysterious to us, though the shape of the mystery is indicated by the sorts of things which our analogies lead us to consider appropriate and inappropriate to God. But God is not completely mysterious: a completely mysterious God would be incredible. It would clearly be intellectually unethical to trust for all things to such a being, and to trust and commend others to him as well. God's being and acting in love imply his thinking, willing, knowing and remembering. Our notions of such processes in a human framework cannot be transferred to God. Yet Christians believe that the corresponding faculties in God cannot be totally dissimilar to those in his creatures, even if we can say nothing of them. Faith affirms that God has intentions, he has personal identity, and that he has risked his identity in relation to men. If we are to say more of God's selfhood, identity and intentions, as characterized by his love, then we must move on to discussion of Christology.

Notes to Chapter 7

1 Persons. cf. P. F. Strawson, *Individuals*, B. Williams, *Problems of the Self* (CUP, Cambridge, 1973), esp. 64ff and 101ff, and art. Persons, by A. C. Danto, in *Edwards, Enc.* op. cit. also P. Bertocci, *The Person God is* (Allen & Unwin, London, 1970); also S. Shoemaker, *Self-knowledge and Self-identity* (Cornell UP, N.Y., 1963).

2 Cosmology, Biology and Theology, cf. I. G. Barbour, *Issues in Science and Religion* (SCM Press, London, 1966) and A. R. Peacocke, *Science and the Christian Experiment* (OUP,

1971). I am indebted to a paper by M. J. Rees given to the Cosmology and Theology Consultation at St George's House, Windsor, in September 1976.

3 On presence, cf. J. Baillie, *The Sense of the Presence of God*, and H. Frei's interesting, *The Identity of Jesus Christ* (Fortress Press, Philadelphia, 1975). cf. H. R. Mackintosh, *The Christian Apprehension of God*. 182ff.

4 cf. *Process Theology*, by J. B. Cobb and D. R. Griffin (lit.) (Christian Journals Ltd., Belfast, 1976) cf. too my review of C. Gunton, *Becoming and Being*, Epworth Review, 1979, 116-7.

5 Thomas. cf. Persson, *Sacra Doctrina*: Anscombe & Geach, *Three Philosophers* (Blackwell, Oxford, 1963). On Analogy in theology, cf. Preller, *Divine Science and the Science of God*, esp. 167f (Princeton UP, 1967).

6 Jüngel, cf. *Gottes Sein* 81f on Gott als Liebe, and *Paulus und Jesus* 211f. cf. *Gott als Geheimnis der Welt* (Mohr, Tübingen, 1977), passim, esp. preface, 408ff of God and love. In der Liebe werden wir aus Habenden Seiende. Denn kann wir sagen, dass Gott die Liebe ist. Als Liebe ist er das Geheimnis der Welt. cf. 298. Gott hat sich am Kreuz Jesu als Liebe definiert.

7 G. Kaufman, cf. esp. *God the Problem*, 7ff, .119ff, and *Systematic Theology* (Scribners, N.Y., 1968) (cf. my review in SJT, 1970, 473-6). For the discussion cf. F. M. McLain in HTR 1969, 1970, 473-76, 155f, D. Griffin in JAAR 41 (December 1973) 554-72, D. Wiebe in Rel. Stud. (1974) 189ff, D. R. Mason in JR 1972, and H. Jones in Rel. Stud. (March 1978), and above all K. Nielsen, *Scepticism*, 73ff (Macmillan, London, 1971). cf. too L. Gilkey, Naming the Whirlwind, and F. Ferre in JR 1972, 286f. On actions cf. too, esp. Judith J. Thomson's excellent *Acts and Other Events* (Cornell UP, 1977) and B. D. Katz, Kim on Events, Phil. Rev. 1978 427f (lit.).

8 cf. Austin Farrer, *Faith and Speculation* (SPCK, London, 1972) and *Reflective Faith*, esp. 178ff.

9 *Pace* Jüngel on the one hand and David Mason and others on the other hand. D. R. Mason, op. cit. cf. B. Mitchell, *The Justification of Religious Belief*, op. cit.

10 cf. Flew and McIntyre, *New Essays*, op. cit., 122ff. (Crombie, Flew, Hare & Mitchell).

11 cf. R. Shaull in *Man in Community*, and T. Rendtorff and H. E. Tödt, *Theologie der Revolution*.

Chapter 8

The Love of God the Creator of Man

1

In thinking about the love of God the creator, it is desirable to give due weight not only to the various structuring elements of Christian thought, catholic and evangelical, on the subject, but to enter fully into the questions raised by the secular mind. A theology which produces answers without listening to questions can scarcely be of service to mankind. It can serve at best only to reassure the particular group of the faithful to which it appeals. In any case, today *our* questions are the secular questions as well as the more traditionally theological questions, and the answers we produce must deal as far as possible with all the questions raised if they are to be helpful to ourselves, not to speak of others perhaps on the fringes of the Christian faith.

In recent theology there has been much discussion of what modern man can and cannot accept, of the problems of cultural pluralism and of secularization. Such discussion is entirely proper and highly relevant. But in dealing with these issues it is important to remember that they have been on the intellectual agenda at least for European theology for at least the last two hundred years. Without constant reminder of the nature of this background, which has important effects on the shape of the present situation, it is too easy to think that ours is *the* generation with unique intellectual agonies to bear. The problems raised by the Enlightenment have not yet been overcome by theology, but they have not yet proved overwhelming, and there is no reason to think that they are entirely insoluble.

Though the patristic, medieval and reformation periods all produced revolutions in theology, it was I suppose the seventeenth century which began to bring about, not everywhere but with increasingly universal significance, a recognizably new situation.

Internal weakness in Christendom was not the least of the factors promoting change. People tired of the endless killing and strife, usually allegedly in the name of Christ, throughout Europe. But at the same time the rise of experimental methods and theories based upon them in the field of natural science, and coupled with this the development of new critical philosophies, threw up questions to which the old theology appeared to provide no satisfactory answers, either in the shape of the Protestant systems of the post-reformation period or the Catholic systems of Post-Tridentine Rome.

The combination of political scepticism and philosophy was itself scarcely new, but here was to have wide repercussions. In the ancient world Lucretius was led by a sense of the folly of strife to abstain from politics, and to attempt to persuade men to free themselves from fear of the gods and of death, a task not of academic importance only, but a practical concern to be stressed as vigorously as possible. The method was worked out in his *De Rerum Natura*, and the goal was the blissful state of *ataraxia*, independence and imperturbability, based on the bonds of friendship. Now new and equally astringent philosophies were to be hammered out.

Bacon and Descartes are perhaps the first names to think of here. Philosophy developed along the two main streams of a rationalist tradition (one thinks of Leibnitz and Spinoza), or an empiricist approach, (Locke), and above all David Hume. Theology where it moved at all tended to pietism, the religion of the believing heart, or to a rationalism which proved useless under the withering attack of man like Hume. The bringing together and mutual critique of rational and empirical philosophies was the contribution of Immanuel Kant. The theological response to Kant was to be worked out most profoundly in the theologian who may justly be called the Father of modern theology (increasingly of Catholic as well as Protestant thought) Friedrich Daniel Ernst Schleiermacher. Along with advances in natural science and in philosophy there had grown up in the late seventeenth and eighteenth centuries an impressive amount of work in historical and literary criticism, and in the interpretation of historical documents. Here work on the interpretation of the Bible was in the forefront of research (Simon, Herder, Lessing, Semler, etc.). This critical work reached a peak in the late nineteenth century (especially in Gunkel and Robertson Smith) but the crucial question had already arisen in the eighteenth century. Is the Bible to be interpreted like any other historical document? If the Fathers and Reformers knew nothing of the new methods (or the new philosophy science etc.) what use were their answers to modern theology? What if history and science were to show that creation stories were not straight descriptive accounts, or that there were mistakes, or many different traditions, in scripture? Was faith then independent of historical events? If so, that was a momentous conclusion. Worse still, if the Fathers and Reformers were demonstrably children of their time, were not contemporary writers equally indebted to their cultures? If all was historically and culturally relative, what of the age old notion of producing THE one correct doctrinal system? It was a measure of the greatness of Schleiermacher that he did not duck any of these questions, but set out to show how Christian faith could be explained in a way that took cognisance of all the new discoveries, and yet was a faithful representation of the meaning of the Gospel, in no sense a sell-out to the fashions of the day.[1]

Sometimes nineteenth-century theology is seen as simply a

continuation of eighteenth-century theology. There were those who carried on the rationalist tradition, e.g. Wegscheider. But the nineteenth century represented also a conscious attempt to solve the problems raised for theology by the eighteenth century, not indeed by ignoring them, but by taking them up, going through them towards a new understanding. Schleiermacher is very much a child of the Enlightenment in one sense, and yet in another he is anything but a child of the Enlightenment. Like Augustine he weaves together many different tunes and that is his genius.

By the time of Schleiermacher as compared with the period of Aquinas or Luther, the intellectual atmosphere had changed. This was not a change which occurred overnight. It had numerous different causes and it happened by infinitesimal steps rather than by sudden revolutions. But theology now found itself in a world that was no longer instinctively a world of faith. There were to be ages of faith to come, say, in the later Victorian period, and even in the period immediately after the Second World War, but these were the product of disciplined relearning of the tradition rather than natural reaction: by 1770, if you like, a pluralistic culture had come to stay. People had to live not in one intellectual community, but in a number of overlapping communities, and these had to be consciously linked to and explained to each other. Schleiermacher was not alone in responding to the changing situation. Gotthold Ephraim Lessing saw with perhaps more clarity than any other eighteenth-century writer the crisis which the Enlightenment produced for Christianity. For this reason he attacked as completely useless, as a mere papering over of the cracks, both the reminders of the old orthodoxy and the synthetic systems of the Neologists, with their easy but vague harmonization of reason and revelation. People like Lessing, and in the next century, Strauss and Overbeck, have performed, of course, a most valuable service to theology, in dispelling the illusion that the problems of theology can be solved easily. In reacting against the old and new rationalisms Lessing moved towards mystical ideas and to Spinoza, and so seemed to be back to the seventeenth-century natural religion. He could see no way from the biblical narratives, from 'accidental truth of history' to 'necessary truths of reason' and vice versa. And yet his battle against all external authorities for the sake of the authority of inner persuasion was a product of the Reformation. Truth for truth's sake was his basic concern, and the good for its own sake. The piety of Nathan the Wise was summarized as dedication to the unconditional will of God and a life of unconditional love. For Lessing the search for truth remains a puzzling task and a hard struggle to the end: there are no elegant syntheses, no easy flowing solutions to the enigmas of religion.

The other seminal figure is Kant. Unlike Lessing, Kant was a man for whom religion was not a vitally important part of life. Kant was very important for Schleiermacher — so much so that it is sometimes thought enough to say of Schleiermacher that of course he was a Kantian, as if that explained all.

Kant's importance for theology was many sided, of course. In the first instance we may say that in the critique of pure reason he had destroyed the old dogmatic systems of rationalism and empiricism, and to that extent gave religion a certain amount of breathing space again. The basic reality lies in the realm of practical reason, which lives out of its own laws, particularly out of the demands of the categorical imperative. Christianity is the historical vehicle for the truth about the moral law, which is itself the expression of the will of God. From religion comes the recognition of the reality of (evil) and its overcoming by good. Interpreted in terms of the moral law, the Bible and the Church could illustrate the truth of the way things are. The result, worked out in *Religion within the Bounds of Pure Reason* (1793) had little of such concepts as grace, but did, in the Lutheran manner, see the law as leading to Christ, and to the understanding of the true self. Kant was particularly concerned with the bounds of religion, but his work, particularly the later *Criti-*

que of Judgement, was to lead to a philosophy of religion in a different direction after his death, when the moment of judgement, or apperception, could be seen as the point of action of the thinking spirit in a different sort of metaphysical framework, in the Romantic view of reason, and so, with little modification, of religion.

Kant is undoubtedly important, yet scarcely a final court of appeal, for modern problems in theology. There are few more unphilosophical moves, in the nineteenth century and in recent writing, than magisterial appeal to the authority of Kant, which often turns out on closer inspection to be founded on nothing more solid than highly eccentric interpretation of one or two random passages taken out of context, with perhaps the odd aphorism from Plato or Aristotle thrown in for good measure.

Against the stress on moral values in Kant and the inadequacies of the systems of the pre-Kantian theologies, Schleiermacher felt it necessary in the first instance to spell out the true nature of religion before he unfolded the nature of Christian religion. Later of course, in the twentieth century a new tack was tried in seeing Christianity as simply the abolition of religion, but this, as we shall see, was to produce its own problems too. We begin with humanity and move to divinity. Religious life involves community from the beginning. The basis of religious feeling is a mystery, (clarity is not everything), religion is a category of its own, the experience of being grasped by the awareness of the universe as a whole: this may seem strange but it is not to be reduced to anything else. This is not an abstract idea but an empirical reality, something from the practical sphere of life. Such a concrete religion receives its most perfect expression in Christianity; this is made clear in the fifth and last of the *Speeches*. The concrete category is realized in specific instances in the positive religions, and particularly in Christianity. A Christianity so arrived at inevitably had a strangely romantic and somewhat vague silhouette. But Schleiermacher was here trying to build bridges, to lead on his educated audience from the less to the more familiar. If this had been Schleiermacher's entire contribution to theology, one might have said that he never really began to overcome the objections raised by Lessing. But part of his genius was that, like Augustine and Aquinas, he moved on to continually new and developed positions.

There was in the Romantic movement a tendency to see the nature of religion as an abstract idea, an idea linked to the achievement of true humanity but essentially part of a larger philosophical framework. In the *Speeches* Christianity hovers between the principle of the truth and the historical particularity. By the time of the *Brief Outline* it is clear that Christian theology is an independent entity, with a life of its own quite apart from any particular philosophical system. This is important to bear in mind in reading especially the *The Christian Faith*.[2]

2

In the last chapter we considered various consequences of the loss of certainty in modern theology, and we have just glanced at the origins of this new situation. To understand more fully we should have to speak of Herder and Hegel, Nietzsche, Feuerbach, Baur, Troeltsch and others. But the basic consequences are clear. No longer can we speak as a matter of course of self-evident truths, far less a single true scheme of dogmatic theology. As we are conscious of living in and attempting to respond to the challenge of a number of overlapping intellectual communities, so the havens of fundamentalism of every sort whether biblical, cultural, religious, conceptual, liturgical or whatever are denied to us, for the simple reason that they will not begin to provide satisfactory answers to our questions. In developing further a Christian understanding of the love of God the creator, I want to deal now with three fundamental issues which make it hard for us to view the world, man and God in terms of conceptual totalities, whether identikit pictures of man, of God or of Christ. These are the issues of cultural relativism, secularization, and the relation of theology to history. I shall examine the consequences for the understanding of God's love of these issues in relation to three selected recent studies which appear to me to raise the problems sharply.

Beginning with the relation of cultural relativity to the understanding of God, Don Cupitt's *The Leap of Reason* provides an instructive attempt explicitly to develop an affirmation of the value of the transcendent out of serious consideration of the manifold consequences of the problem of cultural pluralism.[3] Unlike many essays in the fields of apologetics and the philosophy of religion, this is not simply an attempt to turn philosophical embarrassments into theological virtues. The belief that there is a single structure of truth, whether theological or scientific, has gone. This lack of certainty is itself a threat to a stable structure of reason. Cupitt then examines notions of moral truth, and in particular the relations of truth and power among the officers of religious institutions. The capacity for self-delusion in the notion of subjective truth is set out. A parable is developed, contrasting with Plato's cave, in which a man guesses that there may be a world outside his prison, but without any gap in the wall. This notion that we have no direct knowledge of God is central: 'when I speak of spirituality, I mean the capacity in men for a leap of reason'. Definitions of the transcendent are neither available nor desirable: 'a bony, angular myth, endlessly suggestive and capable of various interpretation, may be of more use.' In religion as elsewhere the patterns in one's mind will decide the truths one will be able to perceive. It is not necessary or desirable to claim any direct intuition of the transcendent. The way of unknowing comes first. So in Christianity the faith is centred mythically upon the history of Jesus, 'a man who lived within the contemporary religious system and at the same time transcended it in his ability to criticize it and see clearly what was wrong with it'. The true religion is the religion which declares itself to be untrue. There have been theologians who have used the phrase 'God reveals himself', but they did so in a fit of absent-mindedness. Theism is justified as a middle way between two kinds of atheism. (The self as pure spirit is the condition of the possibility of freedom and innovation: God as pure spirit is the condition of the possibility of the fellowship of spirits.)

Here we have a welcome affirmation of the problems raised for the tradition by the emergence of cultural pluralism. Theology cannot be done as though nothing had happened. In my own view it is a pity that the insistence throughout that we *can* have no direct knowledge of God leads to the omission of any sort of detailed consideration of claims in the classical Christian tradition both past and present that God has provided some sort of knowledge of himself through faith, even if this is always interpreted knowledge, whether this knowledge has been viewed in terms of revelation, self-revelation, whatever. I would myself regard an acknowledgement of an awareness of God given through Jesus as central and indispensable, however difficult it may be to reach an adequate formulation of the nature of this knowledge. We should not move rather too readily, in the manner we have already discussed, to ontological conclusions of a negative kind, on the basis of purely epistemological considerations.

In taking seriously, as ought indeed to be done, the reality of the problems of pluralism, we must avoid becoming the victim of the way in which we set up the problem. The development of pluralism as an inevitable progression accepts somewhat uncritically the plausibility criteria of the present — 'the old faith' is dismissed as an obviously obsolete monolith. It might be thought that faith may throw up quite as many critical questions as philosophy. In speaking of the transcendent as both grasped solely by a leap of reason, and as a way of coping with relativity we need not neglect other possibilities, e.g. both that some knowledge of the transcendent may be given, necessary or not, and that there may be secular ways of coping with relativity without invoking the transcendent. To suggest that God is, in the end, 'nothing but a fantasy' and to see Jesus as the archetypal critical philosopher of religion, centring his message on 'teasing humour' solves some problems, but raises further ones. For a religion to declare itself to be untrue is not necessarily always a mark of humility, just as to declare one's friends to be unreliable is not necessarily a mark of true devotion. Such a line of argument fails to provide grounds for the affirmation that there is in fact a divine transcendent referent outside the human mind. Without such grounds it appears to me that the justification of belief is not intellectually viable. At the same time, stress on the transcendent as a potential force for the preservation of criticism and freedom in human society remains of course valuable, but for Christians is most specifically understood as part of the fruits of the love of the Creator God.

We should perhaps recall here that though cultural pluralism on a global scale is a new item on the theological agenda, pluralism in itself is as old as civilization. There is perhaps no more successful instance of pluralism in the service of theology than in that most classic of Christian documents, Augustine's *Confessions*. Here the combination of Greek paideia, Ciceronian humanitas and the autobiographical traditions of Roman historiography works to striking and powerful effect. All the tendencies towards religious self-portrayal characteristic of the age, are here, whether in terms of conversion to philosophy in the manner of Synesius, of confession of sin and thanksgiving as in the graceful meters of Gregory of Nazianzus, in the rhetoric of Ennodius or the pure devotion of Paulinus of Nola. Here too is the universal desire for communion with God, typified in Plotinus' Enneads. To this Augustine felt aware of the addition of a new cultural dimension from the Bible, making up what was lacking. 'What shall liberate me from this body of death, but your grace through Jesus Christ my

Lord?' We cannot bring in the old world to redress the balance of the new, but it is worth recalling that our problems are not necessarily in all respects peculiar to our time – provided that we do not escape into the past.

In this connection it should not be overlooked that, in the nineteenth century cultural pluralism produced highly significant conservative[2] as well as liberal reactions, the most interesting of which in this country was the Oxford Movement. Ingenious and sophisticated, Newman and his friends looked scepticism and despair squarely in the face and turned to the consolations of patristic theology and churchmanship, imaginatively updated. If Hurrell Froude were to lapse on occasion into 'contrite reminiscences of a desire for roasted goose, and of an undue indulgence in buttered toast', there was nothing absurd in the development of Newman's theological hermeneutics. Not for the first time or the last, some of the brightest intellects were to find in the past the clues to the present. Their criticism of liberal Protestantism was devastating. But their own programmes took too little account, perhaps, of the history of the present, and so of the future.

3

I have said that there are other, more secular ways of coping with relativity than by invocation of the transcendent. To deal adequately with the manifold issues raised by the phenomenon of secularization would require a large volume in itself. Some mention is however vital, if we are to face the problems of reformulation of doctrine for our own time. It is sometimes imagined that because the 'secular theology' of the 1960s has passed, the problem of secularization has gone away. This is very far from being the case, and all talk of God's love which ducks this issue has serious difficulties. I want to consider in more depth the specific issue of the secular with the aid of what I regard as one of the most fascinating, if one of the most allusive treatments of the subject, Professor Ronald Gregor Smith's last book, *The Doctrine of God*.[4]

We can neither omit the name of God, Smith insisted, nor make free of it. 'The real audacity does not consist in declaring that God is dead, but in daring at all to take that name upon our lips.' Today there is a crisis, not just about a particular doctrine concerning God, but about God himself. A dialogue is required, but not with analytical philosophy, which is not really interested in history. This must involve 'an extension of the proper scope and possibility of human reason to include Christ who is the source of faith' (an interesting contrast to Don Cupitt's programme). Faith is not an isolated phenomenon but is the gift which is given to our situation as an event. Events then, for Smith unlike say Kaufman, are not simply reducible to empirically measurable phenomena. The mystery of God is related to the mystery of man, but not in such a way that 'God' is merely an echo of man's self-understanding, but more as in Calvin's *Dei cognitio et nostri* (a sensible balance between romantic idealism and purist avoidance of the sphere of the human).

In the dogmatic tradition, 'the way faith has been understood has more and more tended to leave out the thrusting confrontation which is at the very heart of faith'. Barth's talk of God is examined, with the aid of Jüngel. God's being is a self-relating being, and this is the primary objectivity of God. Because God's being in itself partakes of relationship, in relations *ad extra* his being can exist ontically. He can relate and be at the same time, and being *ad extra* is the same as being *ad intra*. Both scepticism (being *ad intra* may be different from being *ad extra*, and if so, unknowable) and relationalism (to be is simply to relate and there is no being in itself) are avoided. The criticism of this is that Barth relies on a specific philosophy of being, namely of an inter-trinitarian, self-related, primary and aloof being, to which man and the world can only be related by a positivism of revelation, an ultimately unsupported fideism.

What is needed is a fresh interpretation of God's relation to human existence, and an understanding of man's faith in relation to God as he gives himself to us in history.

There is a way from man to God, and this is grace. Faith involves self-knowledge, which arises in the world, along with other persons. Transcendence is something given in our human experience, in community. This word of encounter is constitutive of man's humanity, and points to a realm of the interhuman. Man becomes a question to himself, which awaits an answer. The answer is the New Testament eschatological message concerning Christ. We can neither abandon transcendence nor preserve it with the concepts of past ages. The historicity of God is understood through the historicity of man, which is in turn based on the word as constitutive of man's humanity. God is involved in our historicity but not simply to be identified with it, not at our disposal but not unknown.

It is necessary to go further than simply providing standard Christian answers to the question of God. It is necessary to produce theology which is not exclusive but builds bridges towards the questions concerning the meaning of human existence, and of human community which men ask. To provide satisfactory answers it is necessary first to listen to the question people ask. Hence the concentration on man in history, asking the question of God for his own existence. God's grace is understood in relation to the human struggle for freedom within the created order. Smith made much more use than Cupitt of the Word as the Augustinian *viva vox evangelii*. But still much more needs to be said of the nature of these key terms grace, man and history in order to provide a more adequate conceptual filling for understanding the nature and activity of God. This is of course the standard weakness of theologies of encounter. But in seeing the problems, the virtues of the existential concern for the word of God in relation to man in history, grace as creating personal community, should not be overlooked.

4

'The aims of history are as diverse as the questions men can ask, and it is an unfortunate, and humourless, truncation of the human imagination to argue that only one kind of history is peculiarly entitled to the name.'[5] Here is the dilemma which faces the theologian who seeks as the Christian theologian must, to understand the relation of the Christian God, for whom to be is to be involved in contingent particularity above all through Jesus of Nazareth, to history.

A good starting point in considering the relation of God to history is as often, the work done by Wolfhart Pannenberg, building on the legacy of Gerhard von Rad. It is worth listing the seven programmatic theses that are the basis of *Revelation as History*.[6]

1. According to the biblical witness, the self-revelation of God has not occurred directly, after the fashion of a theophany, but indirectly through his historical acts.

2. Revelation happens, not at the beginning, but at the end of history.

3. Unlike special manifestations of God, historical revelation is there for anyone who has eyes to see; it is universal in character.

4. The universal revelation of the Godhead of God was not yet realized in the history of Israel, but first in the destiny of Jesus of Nazareth, in so far as the end of history occurs beforehand in him.

5. The Christ event does not reveal the Godhead of the God of Israel as an isolated event, but only as far as it is part of God's history with Israel.

6. The universality of the eschatological self-disclosure of God in the destiny of Jesus was expressed by using non-Jewish ideas of revelation in instruction in Gentile Christian churches.

7 The relation of The Word to revelation is in terms of

prophecy, instruction and report.

Both as a critique of Barth's understanding of The Word and as an exposition of an alternative proposal Pannenberg's work has been ingenious and illuminating. He does not however appear to escape the consequences of Harvey's comment: there may be as many legitimate views of history as there are working historians. His theological concept of history too often represents a conflation of a number of diverse activities in historical and archaeological research, and in particular philosophical traditions. The problem is not solved by relating history to hope and the future. There are obviously endless different sorts of hoping and half-hoping. Ontologies of the future, too, escape none of the thorny metaphysical problems of the present.

Here we find develops a rational theology in which public criteria of rationality are met by the historicity of the resurrection of Jesus. It seems to me that the cumulative case for historicity nowhere reaches the level of probability which it needs to bear the weight which a rationally grounded theology or resurrection would require of it. This is parallel to the choice of 'historicality' as the key to the understanding of man and of 'apocalyptic' as the preferred framework for understanding the complex and often conflicting New Testament narratives. We cannot overcome historical diversity simply by taking thought, however ingenious.

For Pannenberg the transmission of historical traditions is the context from which events derive an intrinsic meaning. The events of the tradition point to and reveal the intrinsic meaning of the Christ event. But traditions can be wrong. Some are, and were, in Israel, the New Testament and the Church. It would seem that the tradition cannot itself say which intrinsic meaning, which interpretation of the tradition, is correct. We must ask how we can test the truth of tradition, who first shaped the traditions, and why. They did not have a tradition to guide them. How do we know whether or not the way in which they shaped the tradition was correct?

5

At this point it is desirable to reflect on the Christian under-taking of man. It is not clear that 'history' as a universal con-cept will take us further towards the understanding of God. But history is human history, and man is for faith uniquely placed at the centre of God's creation. It was not by accident that God became uniquely involved in the contingency of history in the life of a particular man. If we wish to say more of the creator in history, we must make clear what we take to be an appropriate theological account of man. We cannot hope simply to understand God as a mirror image of the human – that would be the romantic illusion. But if theo-logy is for people, then the appropriation of divine revel-ation will be accommodated to human capacity, and God will be understood as the God who is our God.

There is nothing worse than the theologian who knows too much about God and Man, and wallows in the self-congratulation of a blind orthodoxy – unless it be perhaps the theologian who knows too little about God and Man, and drowns his hearers in endless unspeakable wittering about the unsayable – apart that is, perhaps, from the plausible professional who clouds every issue by suggesting that his particular prejudice represents the middle way, where there may be several dozen more or less intermediary ways, between a number of similar but distinguishable ex-tremes. In speaking of man we must try to step carefully be-tween dogmatism and scepticism.

There has been a considerable intensification of interest in recent years in the Christian doctrine of man, in part no doubt because we all find it so embarrassing to talk about God. A year or two ago we had a new and authoritative doc-trine of man, humanity, maturity or human flourishing every six months or so, but now we have gone rather coy and tend to speak of the need to relate modern studies of man to the whole Judaeo-Christian tradition, not to speak of wider cultural history of the human community.

In the various strands of the Christian tradition God is thought to have a purpose for man, and this is often seen as involving the development to the full of his humanity. Improvement in the quality of man's humanity includes improvement in the capacity to give and receive love – in personal relationships among individuals and in relation to society as a whole. This love has often been understood as including involvement, concern, identification, on the basis of and after the manner of the salvation of mankind effected by the love of God in the events concerning Jesus Christ.

Theological talk of man seems then to have included engagement with, and perhaps will continue to include attention to, at least three central issues: (1) the continuing value, if any, of the biblical and traditional heritage of talk about man, (2) the exact cash value of the focus on Jesus Christ in anthropology, and (3) the extent of the pressure to work out a fresh understanding of man in relation to his rapidly changing and perhaps increasingly fragmenting social, cultural and political environment.

We may, of course, also avoid any of the three areas I have mentioned – the third area, say, by embalming ourselves in college port – but I am assuming a certain minimal attention to the real world.

It goes without saying that doctrines of man have, too, important ethical consequences. We are not concerned with being civilized as such – it appears that you have to make considerable advances in civilization before cannibalism becomes socially acceptable. Nor are we concerned with doing what is natural – it's natural for millions to die of hunger, natural for the lower classes to overpopulate the planet, natural for the upper classes to procure discreet abortions. We are concerned, as I understand the matter, with man as he lives and dies, among his fellow men, before God, *coram Deo*.

Man before God, means Christian theology for the Christian community, even theologians' theology. But man among his fellow men, 90 and 9 of whom are outside rather than inside the fold, suggested a comprehensible Christian contribution to thought and action about the nature of the humanity to be hoped for among all mankind, in the context of other religions and increasingly, to my mind, together with people who do not believe in God. If I stick to theologian's theology, it is partly in hope that the problems of the modern world are themselves an integral part of theological concern – we are concerned with public criteria of truth however elusive. I should perhaps recall too that it is possible to say a great deal about the nature of the human, and the Christian doctrine of man, without ever using the word humanity; and conversely it's possible to be savagely inhuman under the slogan of concern for humanity. Words in themselves mean anything: how often have we blanched to hear it said of someone: He's very human, when we realize that what is meant may well be only that he is utterly lazy and incompetent but possessed of a certain meretricious charm.

If we were to send a request around several University departments for a considered answer to the question 'What is man?', we might get some very varied replies, not all of them necessarily polite. Few of these replies would be entirely irrelevant, perhaps, to the task of formulating a Christian doctrine of man – *quicquid homines agunt*, and all that. But here I am concerned primarily with man, Christian and non Christian, as understood in the light of Christian faith. In speaking of man as man of faith I may have, of course, already kicked the ball into my own goal. As Nietzsche put it (*Der Antichrist*, p.77 in my copy, which has a special Aryan introduction): 'The need for faith is a weakness. The man of faith does not belong to himself, he can only be an instrument, he has to be used, he has a need to be used', and so on.

Be that as it may, perhaps I can recall a little of traditional theological interpretation of biblical talk about man. God has created all things, but especially man, for free, dependent obedience to him. Man stands with nature, before God, but has a special status in creation, having dominion and a function of responsibility for his powers. He is created as a social being, male and female, free for the service of his neighbour within the limits of being a creature. Created free for society with God and his fellow men, he experiences a certain contradiction, between the duties of the seminar and the call of the golf course, or whatever. *Nondum considerasti quanti ponderis sit peccatum!* This contradiction has not of course been entirely without its good points. God in human experience has often been present as the one who accepts the unacceptable. A God without grace, perhaps, is a God who is dead. *O felix culpa, quae tantam potuit mereri redemptionem!*

Meanwhile, in Genesis, the springs of contradiction are found in the coils of the serpent, and in the attempt of man, made in the image of God, to become as God, from *imago die* to *sicut deus*. Man's glory as being in the image of God is also his tragedy in seeking to overstep the limits of finite being: he is somewhat given to rebellion, idolatry, pride, whatever, and this disrupts his relations with God and man. The limitations of being, increased by contradiction, are at once accepted and lifted in salvation through Christ.

Much effort has been spent from Israel onwards in debating the meaning of the concept of the image of God. In the Old Testament man is distinguished from other animals by the image of God, in the New Testament Christ *is* the image of God (2 Cor. 4.4., Col. 1.13f etc.). Through the image God's purpose for man of fellowship with God is fulfilled in Christ. But does image of God mean more than this? A great deal of theological capital has of course been made in the tradition out of the alleged distinction between image and likeness of God in the Genesis narrative. Does the image remain when the likeness is lost? How far is restoration through Christ a complete reconstruction, how far a mere renovation? Does the suggestion of some natural inclination towards God detract from the sovereignty of grace? The answer appears to depend on our particular ecclesiological hang-ups! Whatever else, the image of God appears to involve recognition that humanity is not to be improved (and I use the word advisedly) without co-humanity and without God.

How is the theological tradition about anthropology to be related to other sorts of human talk of man? Every schoolboy can trace back the scientific interest in man in the modern period back to the late middle ages, with a new interest in nature and exact observation of natural phenomena, and of man as God's creature.

In 1601 Pierre Charron said that the proper study of mankind is man. Medical science and the keeping of records and statistics brought new perspectives. The average pig doubles its weight in 14 days, the average infant in 180 days – so, man is more sophisticated. (But actually our first infant doubled his weight in about 100 days – no comment.) Man alone can adapt to live in the tropics today and the Antarctic tomorrow, can reflect on himself as being a breeding ground for bacteria or a spiritual being, can create myths and cultures correlated to his physical needs, cooked and uncooked. What is the theologian to make of all this secular anthropology? Is he to dismiss it as of no relevance to theological anthropology, as K. Barth appears to have done? Or is he to produce deep meaning out of truism with the aid of a key theological category as, say, W. Pannenberg has done, *Der Mensch ist seinem Wesen nach geschichtlich*.

Man is by nature an historical character. His distinctive awareness is the awareness of the historicality of his own existence, as a being with a history. But, once upon a time in Israel people discovered that the events of history are to be understood as God's way towards the fulfilling of his promises. The meaning of history is decided by its goal and end in God. As the end breaks in in anticipation in Jesus, the last determination of world history is made. So then, the man who decides for Jesus discovers *par excellence* what it is to be a man, a man with a grasp of the pure meaning of his historical existence. If I come to Jesus, happy shall I be. But what then of God's prophetic word of contradiction of the course of human history, what of the radical hiddenness of God and the scandal of the reality of the cross? Theology is just that little bit awkward.

Back then to the Fathers. Broadly speaking, when one asked oneself in the ancient world what is man, one tended perhaps to speak in psychological rather than in anatomical terms – one spoke about the soul in speaking of man as he really is. This raises of course interesting problems. When does a man acquire his soul? (I say a man, because of course it could be debated in the sixth century whether a woman was in fact a human being or not). Were souls transmitted at conception or specially created by God for each individual? Was the soul better or worse than the body, more or less sinful than body or mind. Luther of course didn't much care for this soul searching – *philosophi et Aristoteles non potuerunt intelligere aut definire, quid est homo theologicus, sed nos Dei gratia, quod bibliam habemus, id possumus* (WA39. 1.179). In their different ways Schleiermacher, Kierkegaard and Bultmann are all children of Luther, building a whole theology of human self-consciousness centred on a doctrine of man as *simul iustus et peccator*, free and inhibited. For Barth on the other hand, or at least partly on the other hand, the proper understanding of man was to be derived solely from attention not to ourselves but to the basic form of humanity shown in the history of the life of Jesus Christ. Through the humanity of God revealed in the humanity of Jesus Christ we may come to understand the true nature of the human. But even Barth recognized on occasion that there must be something in our experience of the human which enables us to recognize a perfection of humanness in Jesus: God creates relationships by invitation rather than by revelatory command.

It may be, as Karl Rahner puts it, that 'Christian anthropology only attains its full meaning when it conceives of man as the obediential potency for the hypostatic union' (though it might be inappropriate to go out and ask a queue of busy shoppers in any supermarket whether they feel they have an obediential potency for hypostatic union).

How can we still have a genuine theological anthropology which is not simply a pale shadow of Christology, but which at the same time takes a realistic view of the ambiguity of the human condition? I rather like some comments on the relation of Jesus to the human from David Jenkins: 'In Jesus Christ we have the demonstration that the true human and personal reality of man is not submerged, defined nor ended by what I can only call the inexplicable and present reality of evil (90). As such, Jesus is the definition of the nature of personalness. And so, you cannot define the reality of man the human person, without taking into account the reality of God.' The hope of man lies in the evidence that the openness we need is offered to us by and as the openness of the love of God. Problems of course will remain whatever we propose. *Non in dialectica complacuit Deo, salvum facere populum suum.*

Interpretations, theological and other, of the nature and destiny of man can be conducted and summed up in numerous ways, in presentations varying from speculative metaphysics to desiccated truism. Poetry and art and innumerable media may contribute to understanding of the human. In theology we are concerned with a doctrine of man which should be neither insulated from nor parasitic upon knowledge derived through other disciplines. We are concerned with man before God, but man in intimate connection with all his fellow men. As such we are bound to have problems with any simple model. How can we produce a single picture of all the men who live, who have lived, who will live, who are and will be with God to all eternity? We must presumably maintain some understanding of the in-built tension between the goodness of God's creation and the reality of contradiction, disaster and evil. We are created to love God and our fellow men, but for various reasons our relationships, though always continuing, become strained. Proper relationships are restored, at least in anticipation, by God in his activity as Father, Son and Holy Spirit. If I were to be permitted here an imaginative restatement of the Christological dimension of the doctrine of man I would want perhaps to say something like this. In Jesus word and history are united in the disclosure of the ultimate meaning of humanity as the capacity to give and receive love, love which always involves speech and action and takes place within the reality of a concrete historical situation. This love is not a bolt from the blue, for we know something of it already, wherever there is goodness done by men. Yet it is in the life of Jesus that we see this love in all its depth, as the disclosure of God whose nature is love, for whom to be is to give himself in relationship to all men. Theology and anthropology are not then mutually exclusive, word and history, nature and grace are not irreconcilable opposites, but everything hangs upon the ways in which they are brought together. For me the clue, as far as there can be a single clue, is love, the love of God, but to speak of God's love is not the end but at best the beginning of a continuing conversation, not an infallible touchstone but perhaps a serviceable signpost.

In conclusion, how can I contribute to human talk of man in a human community of which large sections believe belief in God to be groundless? I suppose perhaps by speaking of a quality of corporate life and corporate concern which, though it derives from God's love, may be hoped to be capable of commending itself in the long run on the basis of its own human credentials, because it reflects the truth of what God has created us to be, and keeps open for us. This has something to do, perhaps, with the Christian's understanding of freedom.[7]

6

It becomes apparent that the understanding of the Christian

God is not to be deepened by a simple 'reading off' of the nature and character of God from an analysis of the character and nature of man. For God is much more than simply a human figure extrapolated to an infinite degree. But it is to man his creature that God has chosen to relate himself in a unique way, and so our understanding of God will be improved by paying attention to all ultimate questions that human culture and enquiry raise, as well as to the biblical narrative and the Church's witness to the Christian Gospel. It is not God in abstract, nor God as man, but God as the creator of man within the context of the created universe with whom we are concerned.

Something more should be said of the love of God as articulated within the structures of creation. It is possible to over-emphasize the relevance of modern cosmological debate for theology. The problem of the relation of creator to creation is posed in a different scale, namely of immensity in relation to the particularity of our world, rather than in a different dimension, by modern awareness of the distances involved in cosmology. These scale differences are present in the same way within our world by the discovery of minute particles in the area of microphysics and microbiology. But the fundamental theological issues remain unchanged. The claims of Christianity in relation to creation remain equally formidable.

To believe in God as maker of heaven and earth is not to have a privileged cosmological theory, but to affirm the sovereignty of God, and the action of his grace in the physical world as well as in personal relations, bringing order into being in the cosmos *ex nihilo*. How this has happened and continues to happen remains ultimately mysterious. The theologian has to affirm that the universe is one, and that the spheres of creation and salvation, nature and grace are complementary and everywhere interrelated. The living God has created life and directs it towards an eschatological fulfilment. For man as creature there is freedom and potentiality for development, but also the possibility of contradiction, alienation, disaster. Both sides of the gift of freedom in creation, fulfilment and disaster, are taken up in God's own involvement in his creation, in the experience of human death and human resurrection, in which God's love for creation is renewed and diversified through Jesus Christ and in the work of God's Spirit in new creation. In speaking of creation from nothing and of corresponding new creation the theologian is using radically metaphorical language. But he is also affirming the truth of the metaphor as God's ultimate spiritual reality, and as the ground of the physical as much as of any mental universe.[8] Talk of the love of God, and indeed any Christian talk of God, is anything but self-explanatory, despite the ease with which theologians are wont to use familiar phrases. On the other hand removing the substance of the Gospel will not solve the problems but only reduce the whole to ultimate triviality. In so far as we are to ground talk of God the creator in history and contingency, it is to consideration of the love of God in Jesus Christ that we must now turn. Creation and reconciliation are not consecutive but simultaneous activities of God.

Notes to Chapter 8

1 cf. K. Barth in *Schleiermacher Auswahl* (Siebenstern Verlag, Munich, 1968) 290ff. cf. H. Frei, *The Eclipse of the Biblical Narrative* (Yale UP, New York, 1975). (Excellent review by A. Macintyre in *Yale Review*, 1976, 251ff.)

2 On Schleiermacher, cf. esp. works by M. Redeker, R. R. Niebuhr and S. W. Sykes.

3 Cupitt, *The Leap of Reason* (Sheldon Press, London, 1976).

4 R. G. Smith, *The Doctrine of God* (Collins, London, 1970), esp. introduction by A. D. Galloway cf. too *J. G. Hamman, The New Man, Secular Christianity*.

5   On the relation of history to the Christian doctrine of God, cf.
    Van Harvey, *The Historian and the Believer* (SCM Press, Lon-
    don, 1967), G. O'Collins, *Foundations of Theology* (Loyola
    UP, Chicago, 1966), P. Carnley, 'The Poverty of Historical
    Scepticism' in S. W. Sykes and J. P. Clayton, *Christ, Faith and
    History* (CUP, 1973), and A. O. Dyson, *The Immortality of the
    Past* (SCM Press, London, 1974).

6   On Pannenberg, cf. G. Klein, *Theologie des Wortes Gottes
    und die Hypothese der Universalgeschichte* (Kaiser, Munich,
    1964), E. F. Tupper, *The Theology of WP* (SCM Press, Lon-
    don, 1974), A. D. Galloway, *W. Pannenberg* (Allen & Unwin,
    London, 1973), cf. my reviews of *Basic Questions I and II* in
    SJT, 1972, 89f, 228f.

7   Man, cf. D. Jenkins, *The Glory of Man* (Allen & Unwin, Lon-
    don, 1973), Pannenberg, *What is Man?* (Fortress Press,
    Philadelphia, 1970), K. Rahner, Theology and Anthropology,
    in *Theol. Investigations*, 9, 28ff, 187ff, and *Hominization*
    (Burns & Oates, London, 1965).

8   cf. I. G. Barbour, *Issues in Science and Religion*, 365f and
    Norman Young, *Creator, Creation and Faith* (Collins, Lon-
    don, 1976).

Chapter 9

The Love of God the Reconciler

1

Christian faith takes its origins from Jesus of Nazareth. This is clear, even to those who think that events in the community of his followers after Jesus' death represent a complete distortion of his life, character and intentions. It is equally clear that interpretations of the significance of Jesus have been and are legion.[1] No single solution is likely to commend itself to all Christians. Where there is a considerable element of residual mystery, it is not given to everyone to agree on the same explanation at the same time. This makes it all the more necessary to spell out Christological proposals in detail, in order through debate and comparison to make progress in deciding upon the basic issues and clarifying these.

Much traditional Christology has been studied under the twin rubrics of the doctrine of the incarnation and the doctrine of the atonement, and the relations between the two. I prefer the concept of reconciliation, stressing again the connection between the life of Jesus and the question of who he was, and the work of Christ, or the nature of the activity of God associated with Jesus.

Let me say something first about doctrines of the incarnation. One of the most interesting moves in recent Christology has been the turn to a so-called 'non-incarnational' Christology as an avenue to progress. It seems to me that this move, as a solution to the problems of Christology, is inadequate. But it is important in pointing to a number of severe difficulties inherent in traditional accounts of Christology, and in posing again acutely such significant questions as the grounds for claims about the finality of Christ.

The love of God is seen to be worked out characteristically in the life, death and resurrection of Jesus Christ. Not all acceptable forms of theistic belief need to be related to Jesus. It is also perfectly possible to produce an amalgam of the beliefs of different religions in which Jesus Christ occupies a peripheral but still distinctive place. Such syntheses could doubtless perform important social functions in providing suitable mythological frameworks for reconciling differing belief systems. Reconciliation between peoples is certainly part of the ongoing task of the humanization of mankind. The question, however, is whether Christian faith is more accurately expressed by insistence on a unique incarnation of God in Christ in a strict and highly particular sense.

2

Since the Enlightenment at least, traditional theories of both incarnation and atonement have posed considerable intellectual problems. While mainstream Christianity has adapted variations of traditional themes, in more or less liberal proposals, very many other thinkers, less familiar, espoused much more radical options, notably in various forms of deism. In such communities as masonic groups, which have their origins, at least in their modern forms, in post-Enlightenment philosophies, non-incarnational Christologies have long been acceptable as standard, without upsetting the framework of religious belief and observance. So masonic teaching could speak of Christ as a prophet, equal to other prophets, with difficulty, and indeed as a significant affirmation of belief.

The development of the Socinians in the sixteenth and seventeenth centuries, and the advances made by unitarian spirituality in the nineteenth, bear eloquent witness to the coherence, rationality and indeed the religious efficacy of non-incarnational theologies in life, thought and worship. The question is whether such interpretations are most true to the state of affairs indicated by the Christian Gospel. It is not of course necessary to adopt a Unitarian confession in order to incorporate the substance of unitarian beliefs. The first Unitarian chapel in Britain was started in 1773 by a dissenting Anglican priest, and in the nineteenth century large sections of the Presbyterian Church in England and the Congregational Church in America adopted Unitarian beliefs.

In this country, particularly in Anglican theology over the last hundred years, great stress has been laid on the doctrine of the incarnation as *the* main support of Christian doctrine.[2] If the doctrine of God could be left safely to philosophers, and doctrines of the spirit to ecclesiologists, Christology and in particular the incarnation has been the focus, and often, it seems, the sum of doctrine. This focus, whether in realist or idealist framework, has been a valuable stimulus to Christian social concern. Where a theologian like Barth, who has also been concerned with incarnation, has stressed transcendence, much English theology has been particularly concerned with immanence. It comes then in one sense as no surprise to find the search for new patterns turning away from immanence to transcendence, to what has been termed a 'non-interventionist' notion of God.[3] We appear at first sight to be again in the proximity of particular forms of deism, a position which has been found attractive since the Enlightenment for a number of good reasons. If coherence, economy and clarity are our main requirements, then incarnation does not appear to be a very good model for Christology. However the recent debate throws up a number of useful clues to the understanding of the role of the love of God in Christology.

The love of God is expressed through Jesus in an act of complete divine self-giving which is also perfect self-affirmation. The focus, as I see it, is upon neither incarnation nor atonement, but upon a series of actions and events involving life and death, resurrection and renewal. I want to begin by summing up the shape of my proposal, anticipating and indicating the general direction of the reasoning which follows. This is basically a continuation of the programme outlined in chapter one. I begin from a position of affirmation of Christian faith. But I shall want to distinguish carefully the strands of description, explanation and recommendation in the argument.

3

Jesus of Nazareth was a particular individual who lived in a particular place at a particular time. He lived within the historical, and cultural conditions, possibilities and limitations of his environment. This the historian can affirm, and the theologian is glad to agree. That he lived, a man among men, may be regarded as an historical fact. Theology is not improved by the re-writing of history. It is true that the Jesus who emerges from the New Testament was a man who did some very extraordinary things, who had a powerful influence on people. But this does not in principle distinguish him from other men who have made their mark on history. He was a man, not some sort of impersonal or representative humanity, not less or more than human but simply human. That he was human, of one substance with us according to his humanity, even the Chalcedonian definition could affirm, indeed was concerned to affirm at a time of pressure to lose everything in his divinity. What is it to be human is a question of great complexity. Jesus may well also have been, as Karl Barth has put it, the basic form of humanity. That is an attractive theological proposal to which we shall return. But first of all he was a human being with all that this entails for actions, thought, emotions, limitation, potential.

The theological implications of Jesus' particular humanity have been well brought out in two twentieth-century Christologies, D. M. Baillie's *God was in Christ*, and J. A. T. Robinson's, *The Human Face of God*. Baillie saw the strength of incarnation as lying in great part in the emphasis that God was, really, concretely involved in all the risks and uncertainties of particular occasions in human history. This led him to stress the individual and complete humanity of Jesus, despite the theoretical advantages offered by patristic concepts of anhypostasia, or impersonal humanity.[4] John Robinson's work spells out in careful detail the sociological and pyschological implications of being human, writing in conscious opposition to Victorian theories which often, even in liberal Christologies, failed to draw important implications of human individuality. To make Jesus less than human is to confuse the issue insolubly.[5]

It is not clear however that we necessarily make Jesus less than human by affirming that he is also the Son of God. It may, of course, be observed that if Jesus, in any degree however limited, transcends the limits of empirical humanity as we observe this in ourselves and others, this is docetism. But if it fails to affirm that Jesus is in a unique sense one with God, then our Christology will not be 'from below' but will remain below, producing further complications. Here we face the paradox, mystery or muddle, depending on how one sees it, which Christological discussion inevitably raises. If Jesus is more than we are, in any sense, this is docetism, and he can do nothing for us. If Jesus is no more than human, and we need God himself to bring us salvation, then we are not saved, there is no reconciliation.

One favourite area for consideration as evidence of the 'more than human' element in Jesus is to affirm his sinlessness. Many theologians, in other respects fairly liberal in their theological sympathies, have stressed Jesus' sinlessness as that which gives his moral character its uniqueness and its authority. Some classical theologians argue that Jesus never knew what it was to suffer real temptation, a view which seems strange to our modern moral consciousness. Much depends, too, on what we mean by sin. Robinson has stressed the element of sexuality in Jesus' humanity, an area sometimes thought of as sinful and therefore to be excluded in Jesus. Jesus on the other hand also presumably must have been involved like all human beings in the social sins of his own culture, having where others thousands of miles away had not, but these can scarcely be seen as direct responsibilities. Again, it would be odd if Jesus had never been naughty as a child. Still, we may say that that is not what we mean by sin.

If we say that Jesus appears not to have been sinful in that he never in fact behaved in a morally reprehensible way, we are perhaps coming closer to the point. We do not mean that he was never angry or the like. But if it were to be shown that for example he deliberately lied to his disciples for his personal advantage, or handled money dishonestly, then this would certainly count in a most telling way against the truth claims of the Christian faith. Integrity at this level is necessary, but not sufficient, for establishing Jesus' special sort of human excellence. We have to look elsewhere, perhaps at the notion of a life of complete trust in God and complete selflessness in acting for his fellow men, rather than at an area of quasi-physical incapacity to sin, in speaking of his special character.

Jesus was clearly a most remarkable and impressive human being. If he had been a mere nonentity, a cypher for the action of the hidden God, he would not have impressed people as he did. He need not be thought of as more impressive than all other impressive people, but clearly he was impressive. He showed concern, loving concern for other people in his actions, and he spoke of the quality of God's concern in his teaching. It is often said that his actions explained his teaching. But equally, his teaching explained his action; these were complementary. And, of course, a teacher may act decisively precisely through his teaching.

It is usually in speaking about the divinity of Christ that people have spoken of his relationship to God. Yet this relationship is also of basic significance for the understanding of his humanity. Jesus was an orthodox Jew who was utterly devoted to the worship of Israel's God. To say this is already to say a great deal. True, he was radically critical of large areas of contemporary piety in theory and practice, but this did not detract from his devotion to God. This passion for God was what decisively shaped his thought and action.[6]

It would be convenient to have a series of autobiographical reflections from which we could learn of Jesus' thoughts, his impressions of the events in which he was involved from day to day, his theological jottings.[7] Unfortunately we possess nothing of the kind, we have no way of access to his private reflections. On the other hand, we need not suppose that there was a serious discrepancy between what he thought and what he said and did. His thought is reflected in his actions. Though his unique relationship to God may well have involved a unique consciousness of God, we are in no position to say anything about this. But his words and actions, as far as we know of them, demand special attention.

Here as elsewhere we shall not enter into the details of biblical interpretation. An historico-critical approach to the issues is however everywhere presupposed. In view of the diversity in the biblical material and the technical problems involved in interpretation, I rely exclusively and unrepentantly on the judgements of specialists in the biblical field, in so far as I have been able to take full advantage of these.

4

If the events concerning Jesus suggest that God is involved as both the subject and the object of Jesus' life of discipleship, then the life and teaching of Jesus reflect in an important sense the activity of the Godhead, which culminates in participation in death while not being overcome by death. This need not mean that our concepts of God are bound for ever to the imagery used by Jesus,[8] any more than the fact of his having chosen men as his disciples binds us to the subordination of the role of woman in the Christian community. These are the limitations consequent upon taking the risk of incarnation. It does mean however that certain structuring elements of Jesus' life remain central to our understanding of God and man. This implies that it is possible to extract continuing elements from culture-bound activities, a point much disputed.

Our concern here is with the understanding of the nature of God's love in relation to the life, death and resurrection of Jesus Christ. We are not, it seems to me, called upon to defend the concept of incarnation *per se*, far less to make an absolute choice between ontological and functional Christologies and the like. We are concerned with a true understanding of God's love in the events concerning Jesus. Sometimes it has been possible, as Otto Weber has done, to see the history of phases of Christological discussion as the conflict between a one-sided theology of incarnation and a one-sided theology of the cross.[9] At other times the conflict appears to lie between incarnational and non-incarnational, between metaphysical and moral frameworks. There are good reasons for choosing between one or other of these options in particular cases. But the primary foci of attention remain the life, the cross and the resurrection of Jesus, the significance of the three being always interrelated.

Life, death, resurrection; let us consider what is involved here. Jesus was a Jew who lived in the Middle East, of the male sex, belonging to what in modern jargon might be termed the lower middle classes. Our knowledge of the sort of person he was is spelled out in the sorts of things he did, in the people with whom he associated, the decisions he took, the directions in which he moved. He was a religious man, devoted to God and his fellow men yet coming into conflict with religion and politics, with Church and State. His actions were paralleled by his teaching. He taught the imminent coming of the Kingdom of God, and connected this with a decision for or against himself and his mission. Characteristically he taught in parables. Many of these parables were concerned with the nature of the Kingdom, and were later to be referred to himself, though Jesus did not make this explicit connection. Much that he said and did, his recommendations for the conduct of his followers through his words and his personal example can be seen in parabolic terms, as pointers, indicators accompanied by the weight of his own authority. Yet not everything was in parabolic terms, e.g. the Sermon on the Mount, and it would be inappropriate to look for any such simple key to understanding. Jesus lived and taught, he forgave sins, it appears, in the place of God, he was executed. He died condemned as a traitor and a heretic, though he was what we could call today a man of the highest integrity and compassion, and he experienced more suffering than most, dying for his God. There is no need to believe that he was an intellectual giant, a perfect athlete or that he possessed all the human qualities par excellence. Despite what is often said, his life and death do not on the face of it 'make sense' of the world in which we live, except to underline a facet of human cruelty. He clearly might not have been the life and soul of every party. He died, but others have died for their faiths, and equally horrible deaths.

It is however particularly in the context of what came before and what came after that the life and fate of Jesus took on a new significance, however we may evaluate that significance. Jesus worshipped Israel's God, the creator of heaven and earth. For Jesus too this God was the creator God, who would always be with his people. Israel recognized the contradiction in human nature between what is and what should be, and looked to God to send a messiah to give men new hearts and to renew the covenant. It appears that Jesus saw in his own mission both the fulfilment and the radical transformation of the covenant. He brought forgiveness and renewal. In him God's love was brought again to men, in all that he did. He spelled out the meaning of God's love in concrete situations. But still, he died.

5

What are we to make of the death of Christ? Doctrines of 'the atonement' have taken numerous forms in the history of Christianity, and, as has often been pointed out, none of the explanations has ever become the standard explanation. Differences here have produced radically different theologies. Ernst Käsemann for example has devoted a well known essay to showing that for a theology with the centre in the phrase: *crux sola nostra theologia*, any attempt to put the cross in a series with creation, incarnation and resurrection is already a flat contradiction of the initial emphasis.[10]

What difference does it make for theology that Jesus died condemned on the cross rather than in bed in extreme old age, after a life of benevolence and constructive statesmanship in the pursuit of the welfare of his countrymen? For some versions of theology, it makes little ultimate difference. Jesus was a man who lived in devotion in God, and set an example of this devotion and its ethical consequences for all time to come.[11] Jesus was the man in whom God showed decisively his devotion for his creatures. This could have happened without the crucifixion. It might be suggested that Jesus' death was a final demonstration that God loves men however they may hate his messengers. Another conclusion is that on the cross God died, and so today we have theology after the death of God. Numerous further possibilities exist. It may be thought that the supreme characteristic of God's love is self-giving, and so Jesus, in whom God was at work, had to die for mankind. But then it is not

clear why love should not normally be thought to be expressed in positive affirmation, in creation of the fullness of
life, in the biblical imagery, rather than in bitter sweet, sad
and beautiful failure, not to say highly unpleasant ex-
ecution.

Lutheran theology speaks of the message of the cross, and
often feels that such a notion has almost disappeared from
Protestant theology in the English speaking world. It is not
always clear however what that message is. One major component of theologies of the cross has been the theme of
judgement, a concept much criticized since the Enlightenment. What sort of moral sense does it make to assert that
on the cross God judged humanity for its self-centredness
and Jesus' death accepted and lifted this burden from us?
The young Schleiermacher was not the first or the last to
find such notions intolerable. Variations on judgement,
based on classical theories of satisfaction and substitution,
have been thought by some to be theologically vital, by
others to be morally intolerable. Here there are conflicting
doctrines of man. It is often suggested, too, that the main
objection today to theories of justification and sanctification
in relation to judgement is not so much their theological inadequacy as their plain incomprehensibility in the modern
world: a theology is only as good as its capacity for real
illumination.

Perhaps the most impressive modern restatement of the
theme of judgement in relation to the cross is in the theology
of Karl Barth, for whom the relation of incarnation to
atonement is worked out in an interpretation of the parable
of the prodigal son. The judge of the world himself takes our
place, is judged in our place, and at the same time brings
deliverance from the evil which is destroyed in judgement
through raising Jesus Christ from death. But this reconstruction is often regarded as a moving piece of poetic meditation
which is basically irrelevant to Christology today. The same
critique would apply to the similar and derivative imagery
used by Hans Urs von Balthasar.[12]

Further theories have been based on sociological observation of cults of dying and rising Gods in the ancient world
and in a number of recent cultures. They may also be
evolved in relation to particular philosophical requirements.
In the 'mediating' theologies of nineteenth-century Germany
it was deduced that for the divine love to give himself to us,
for the absolute to be involved in immanence, it was
necessary for God to involve himself in an incarnation which
should continue to the point of atoning death, out of which
came newness of life. Such a philosophical deduction of the
absolute necessity of the cross has its attraction, but it is not
necessarily the best interpretation of that which concerns the
biblical narratives.[13] In the New Testament the cross is a
sheerly contingent fact. It just happens, showing the depth
of human callousness. It explains, partially, not the nature
of God but the nature of man. And the sequel in the resurrection of Jesus increases rather than clarifies the mystery of
God.

6

If the cross furnishes us with no explanations, what are we to
make of the resurrection of Jesus? It is clear that understanding of the cross must take cognisance of what came before
and after. The love of God is not likely to be understood
satisfactorily simply in terms of self-sacrifice, even though
this may be one indispensable element. But introduction of
understanding the resurrection may be thought only to com-
pound the difficulties. If there is disagreement about the
cross, at least it is not usually denied that Jesus died. But it is
not always agreed that a resurrection took place, or what
such a happening could be. It could even be argued that the
resurrection of Jesus, however understood, is less central to
understanding God's love than his death. There is talk of
resurrection of the dead in the Old Testament, to which
Jesus' resurrection adds nothing of substance.

For the New Testament writers, Jesus' death was not only the end of his life but the beginning of a new life for him, and through him for all men. To them, something appeared to have happened which transformed his followers into men who believed that God had raised Jesus from the dead, who believed that through the Spirit they were able to worship the risen Christ as God. These convictions took place only slowly. Evidence for this transformation is in no sense a complete proof for any particular resurrection theory. But the transition from despair to confidence, though susceptible of more than one explanation, remains a remarkable factor in the complex resurrection situation.

What exactly happened to the body of Jesus we are never likely to be in a position to say; decisive evidence does not appear to exist. From the historian's point of view it is contingently possible that a skeleton could in the future be found and shown to be that of Jesus. It cannot be proved that the tomb was empty on the third day, and the stories, like much of the biblical narrative, bear evidence of theological reconstruction. But some of the evidence supports the tradition, a state of affairs affirmed both by those who regard the tomb as theologically secondary and those who stress literal facticity.

To say that the tomb was empty is by no means yet to be able to establish that God raised Jesus from the dead to sit at his right hand in heaven. The tomb may have been emptied by 'a person or persons unknown'. If this was done by agents of his opponents, it is odd that they did not use the fact to their advantage in quashing the myth of resurrection. This is perhaps the most mysterious area of Christian faith, and no explanations are entirely satisfactory. If God by some mysterious process literally raised the physical body of Jesus, where did Jesus then physically and openly go to? Heaven is not a spatiotemporal location. Reference to the doctrine of ascension, in which it may be affirmed that Jesus remained in our world in an exalted state for a period before final translation to heaven, does nothing to resolve the problem.

Within the metaphorical range of language, between the strictly literal and the strictly mythological, we have to talk about a spiritual reality which is virtually inconceivable.

Experience of the presence of the risen Christ, in the period of the so-called appearances and in the early Christian community, has been variously described as existential encounter, psycho-physical hallucinatory experience and the like. Accounting for one area of the problem raises new difficulties in another. At least we can rule out the accounts based on the supposition that Jesus did not die but fainted on the cross, was taken down in error and then recovered, favoured in earlier generations but ruled out by modern acquaintance with the medical engineering of crucifixion.

What precisely happened it is impossible to be sure. It is not in principle impossible that an entirely unique event occurred, in which God raised Jesus from the dead, in order to be identified with himself in a spiritual entity in a manner quite beyond our comprehension. This would not rule out the possibility that the bones of Jesus may still lie buried in Palestine. It does rule out the suggestion that the event of the resurrection is constituted by the subjective experience of believers alone. Human response remains human response. But human response to a spiritual reality need be no less objective than to a physical reality.[14]

For Christianity, the love of God which is characterized in the biblical narratives by its constancy promises a continued existence beyond the contingencies of this life. The quality of this future is related directly to the life and fate of Jesus. In this context and framework it is not irrational to respond to the resurrection narratives by supposing that here some unique occurrence took place in making the transition from death to new life. This is an affirmation of faith, which does not amount to any sort of proof. It has however some further rational grounds. The results of the crucifixion included visions of the risen Christ, though these were the exception rather than the rule. More usually there was experience of faith, understood as experience of the presence of the spirit of God, or the spirit of Christ. There was affirmation of the forgiveness of sins. Jewish piety had spoken of sin and its expiation through keeping the law. Jesus spoke of the need for forgiveness and granted this in the place of God, a process not unnaturally regarded as anti-social. The forgiveness experienced in the community was understood as the forgiveness of Jesus Christ. This too is part of the specific meaning of the resurrection.

It should not be forgotten that the considerations examined earlier concerning God's acting in contingent events on particular occasions applies with full force to understanding resurrection. There is no royal road, no cutting the Gordian knot. But it was indubitably on the basis of reflection upon the series of life, death and resurrection, however difficult, that men decided then, and decide now, that God was in Christ reconciling the world to himself.

The inference that God raised Jesus from the dead is a theological judgement, which takes account of the available historical evidence. Other factors involved are our understanding of the life and death of Jesus in relation to the God of Israel, and Christian experience of God since that time. To affirm the resurrection of Jesus is not to resolve a mystery, but to make a recommendation about its nature and implications.

The resurrection is a vital part of the evidence for the claim that God's love is not only a self-giving love but precisely therein a self-affirming love, effective in bringing new life out of death. This movement from death to life is part of the structure of the unfailing quality of God's love, often despite appearances. The love of God in reconciliation comes to men through the life, death and resurrection of Jesus, through incarnation and atonement equally. That element of reconciliation traditionally expressed in incarnation takes place in the death and resurrection as much as in the life of Jesus. That element traditionally expressed in atonement takes place in the life as much as in the death and resurrection of Jesus.

Notes to Chapter 9

1 cf. Sykes and Clayton (eds.) op. cit. *Christ, Faith and History* (CUP, 1973).

2 cf. Gore, *The Incarnation of the Son of God*, H. S. Scott-Holland, in *Logic & Life*, London, 1885, *Lux Mundi* ed. Gore (John Murray, London, 1881).

3 cf. on Schleiermacher and G. Kaufman above, cf. Wiles, *The Remaking of Christian Doctrine* (SCM Press, London, 1974).

4 Baillie, *God was in Christ* (Faber, London, 1948).

5 Robinson, *The Human Face of God* (SCM Press, London, 1972).

6 As Pannenberg, KuD 1975/3, 160f. cf. 'The danger of a short circuit in a Christology from below lies in this, that it wants to begin with the humanity of Jesus in differentiation from his relationship with God.' cf. too R. R. Niebuhr, *Experiential Religion*, 130f. 'When Jesus so appeals to men, he does so as a God-shaped person. Without God he vanishes as a concrete personality.'

7 On the quest of the historical Jesus, cf. H. Anderson, *Jesus* (Prentice-Hall, New Jersey, 1962), G. Bornkamm, *Jesus of Nazareth*, H. Tödt, *The Son of Man in the Synoptic Tradition* (SCM Press, London, 1965). cf. recent discussion on the difficult but representative 'Son of Man' problem in J. St. N. T. 1.(1978) 4-33.

8 cf. my *Hilary of Poitiers: A Study in Theological Method*, op. cit. 179f.

9 cf. O. Weber, *Grundlagen der Dogmatik* I, Vorwort (Neukirchener Verlag, 1962).

10 cf. E. Käsemann, The Pauline Theory of the Cross, *Interpretation*, 24 (1970) 151ff. cf. J. Knox, *The Death of Christ*, 147f. The early Church did not think that the purpose of Christ's death was to reveal God's love.

11 As J. Hick, etc., cf. Machovec, *A Marxist Looks at Jesus* (DLT, London, 1976).

12 Barth cf. esp. paras. 59 and 64 of C.D. (4.1 and 4.2) Balthasar. cf. my comments in Erasmus 1978, 209f.

13 cf. C. Welch, *God and Incarnation in Mid-nineteenth Century Thought* (OUP, 1965), R. Holte, *Die Vermittlungstheologie* (Almquist, Uppsala, 1965).

14 On the resurrection, cf. Lampe and Mackinnon, *The Resur-*

rection (Mowbray, London, 1966), Cupitt, *Christ and the Hiddenness of God* (Lutterworth, London, 1971), esp. O'Collins, *The Easter Jesus* (DLT, London, 1973), *The Significance of the Resurrection for Faith* (SCM Press, London), ed. with introduction by Moule (Marxen, Wilkens, Delling and Geyer). cf. Rahner TI 9.208. 'The moment we picture to ourselves a dead man returning once more into our temporal dimension, with the biological conditions belonging to it, we have conceived of something which had nothing whatever to do with the resurrection of Jesus, and which cannot have any kind of significance for our salvation either.'

15   cf. M. Dummett in *New Blackfriars*, Nov. 1977.

Chapter 10

Love and the Nature of Salvation

1

In speaking of salvation through Christ we are talking about the centre of the Christian Gospel, and it is important to say something clear and positive about it. But there are many different ways of looking at salvation, many different estimates of the issues involved. No single account is likely to satisfy everyone. Still, there remains the task of attempting to spell out constructive approaches and giving them detailed expression. It is possible to lay great stress on the complexity and insolubility. But that may be on occasion to avoid the material issues. It is possible to over-simplify by some sort of leap of faith. But that is often a counsel of despair. What I want to do here is to set out what I consider to be a reasonable approach to the subject, taking account of some major objections to my argument as they arise.

It would be idle for me to pretend to come to the subject of salvation through Christ with an entirely blank mind. I know that for millions of Christians through the ages these words have been perfectly well recognized and understood as referring to the central nucleus of the Christian faith – to the fact that for those who have faith, however strong or weak, the central purpose of their lives is believed to have been fulfilled, to be fulfilled and to be further fulfilled in the future through the advent and continuing presence of Christ in the world. Who is this Christ? He is the anointed one of God the creator of the universe. If there is one Jesus and there are many Christs, still, the many constitute the bridges between the particular man Jesus who lived and died and the transcendent creator of the universe. For some this subject matter is more a quest, for others more a find, an assured discovery. For many sometimes more the one, sometimes more the other.

Let me begin this chapter with a preliminary survey of concepts of salvation. Salvation has had all sorts of meanings in the course of its journeys around the byways of the history of doctrine, and has developed its character by association with all sorts of other conceptual frameworks. People have thought of salvation as rescue and restoration, as revelation and reconciliation, as representation and substitution, judgement and making righteous, incarnation and atonement, decontamination from the things of this world and attainment of a heavenly realm, something almost in the shape of a consumer durable and accompanied by prosperity, liberation, justice and the establishment of specific forms of social and political orders, and so on.

In the past as in the present, there have been all kinds of spin-off from the fusion and confusion of theological and non-theological usages. But in the theologies of all theistic religions salvation, however further explained, has always been held to have its origins in God, and this is particularly the case for Christianity, to which I shall confine myself here.

Salvation is from God. God's salvation is God himself, but salvation is through Christ. Christ is God, and God, perhaps, is Christ. Problem solved, or rather dissolved. How much of God, or indeed Christ, is involved in our salvation and how? We have a number of undetermined primary concepts here, which can be spelled out in a large variety of ways in relation to each other. What do we understand by salvation, by Christ, by through, and above all, by God? The last of these is by far the most diversely contested even within Christian theology and the most crucial. But we shall want to limit ourselves as severely as possible to the soteriological motif.

It is a commonplace that in the history of doctrine there was little attempt to enforce a single framework of soteriological orthodoxy in the manner of frameworks of Christological orthodoxy. Dividing the imagery into two main groups, we find reference to salvation as primarily rescue from some great evil, corresponding to a generally pessimistic doctrine of man, in the tradition of Paul, Augustine and Luther, and imagery referring primarily to a positive fulfilment of the goal to which man is naturally inclined by his creator, in the tradition of Irenaeus, Origen and the Renaissance. Both lines have advantages and disadvantages and can be read to emphasise these according to taste. Modern theologians usually attempt to take account of the advantages of each, stressing on the one hand the reality of human freedom and the dignity of man, and on the other the reality of the gulf between human frailty and the goodness of the transcendent God, and the assurance of grace to all men. Whatever the philosophical difficulties, it has usually been felt necessary to deny both Pelagianism and determinism, synergism and cynicism. But it is one thing to affirm and deny, and another thing to provide good rational explanations.[1]

In theology everything is related to everything else. This need not incline us to espouse a particular theory of the understanding of reality as totality, or anything of the sort. But it does mean that we shall have to come back again to the primary words like God and Christ. Here we begin however with the theme of salvation. I turn first to the negative theories, to a sort of counterfactual soteriology. If it had not been God's salvation, then we should have been overwhelmed.

This salvation has sometimes been seen as a cosmic victory over an evil force, sometimes as the healing of a disease. The unassumed is the unhealed. But it is not necessary for the case worker to become completely identified with his or her

charge in order to be of assistance. Indeed such absorption
might well prove fatal for both. It is not necessary for us to
imagine that God himself had to come into our world and to
take human flesh in order to redeem us, especially if our
salvation is not to be conceived of exclusively as deification.
Nothing is necessary for God — he could have saved us in any
way he pleased, if indeed he has saved us. It is sometimes
said that God who is love had to come into our human pre-
dicament, to experience and to act from within our condition. But this, it may be argued, is excessive anthropomorphism: a transcendent God does not need to add to
his experience.[2] Still, the notion that God himself is intimately involved with us in saving us from destruction remains a powerful support to Christian faith. But the
sufferers still die. Perhaps God too has died. He does not,
perhaps cannot, prevent disasters in this world. And yet,
Christians do not claim immunity from physical death.[3]

I turn now to the more positive accounts. Salvation is the
goal to which men have been directed from the beginning of
their creation. Here the coming of Christ is often seen in the
first instance in terms of the importance of his life and
example. As a man he brings God's message to his fellow
men, transforming the law of Israel. Become what you are,
act in freedom as Jesus acts in freedom and you will inherit
the kingdom of heaven. This is splendid advice and sometimes we take it. But there are all too many circumstances in
which this will to action is precisely what is lacking. Here the
promise of a path to perfection receding into the eschatological distance may become a counsel not of hope but of
despair. Once again, the good news becomes bad news. On
the other hand, the presence of crushing difficulties should
not in itself lead us to despair entirely of human progress,
fragile and precarious though that progress may be. The
path along the *ordo ad Deum* includes the accompanying
presence and hope of the creator himself.

We see again the difficulty of the theological enterprise. It
is only too easy to confuse programmes with results, and yet

it is highly desirable to put up a well considered theory. I ought perhaps to say something again about my understanding of God, if only in a condensed manner, before talking further about salvation.

Too often theologians simply assume that God is some sort of known factor, revealed or hidden, predictably unknown or predictably and privately disclosed. We bring all kinds of hidden and comforting assumptions from traditions we purport to have discarded into our talk about the God of a thoroughly modern theology, and we sit secure on the ghosts of our sawn off branches – as it were. Clearly there can be naïve anthropomorphism in assertions equally about the knowability or the unknowability of God. No less trying is the 'my God is more unknowable than your unknowable God, but infinitely more accessible than your accessible God' gambit, which falls easily into the tedious assumption that I am the only person who has actually got the God concept right.

I have suggested that Christian concepts of God involve salvation through Christ as a core element. It is not always desirable to emphasize the element of salvation in speaking of God the creator, and over-emphasis has its dangers. But where the salvific motif is left out, concepts of God are less than adequate to the truth of the way things are, and most worthwhile things in theology as in all life have their risks.

2

Something more should be said here about the Person of Christ in relation to his work and the problem of human fulfilment. According to my understanding of God as love, to be God is among other things to give oneself in such a way as to enable mankind to give itself without restraint, to destroy alienation from within. This movement is spelled out for us in ways which we could not have discovered for ourselves in the story complex of the biblical narratives. All our language about God, like our talk of other minds, contains a large element of metaphor. But it is not all totally analogical. In the parabolic structure of these narratives it is suggested that God freely chooses to involve himself in human life and death, and overcomes death in the raising of Jesus. To be God is to be involved in creation and providence, in the life, death and resurrection of Jesus, in the manner indicated by trinitarian models of a self-related being, father son and spirit. This is neither an exhaustive description of God nor simply a piece of mythology, but a model for faith with a complex logic. Such an account is at best the beginning rather than the end of a conversation, but it is decisive for my interpretation.

The point has often been made that it was not necessary for God himself to be involved personally in a unique identification with the man Jesus in order for Jesus to bring us the message of God's love, or indeed for God to make that love effective. Arius was probably no fool, and the case for some sort of version of a 'non-incarnational' Christology is considerably stronger than is often assumed. The choice can be made to appear clear cut, but I fancy it is not. Incantations about substance, divinity and incarnation in themselves will get you nowhere; in theology there are no magic words. All depends on the precise context and the nature of the particular instantiation. It is not unknown for incarnation language to obscure what is precisely the main thrust of the concept, namely intimate involvement in all the problems risk and contingencies of human history, and to lead to a flight from reality, human and divine.[4] In the same connection, Christological distinctions between similarities of degree and of kind, and procedures from above and from below, and the like, can scarcely be determined by linguistic considerations. It may be possible to suggest a similarity of degree so great that it becomes one of kind or substance, and identity of substance need not always indicate identity like that of lumps of clay from the same pit.

If in Christ we have to do with the transcendent God, then our Christology will always be in a sense from above, and since none of us can speak God's language, we must always work from below.

David Jenkins has said that 'The object and effect of "Arian-type" arguments is to keep apart the divine and fulfilling reality in its unique real and full sense from the material and historical which is the arena of human activity and hope. The direct and unmediated presence and activity of God in the world as we know it, live it and are part of it, is denied. But this is to tell a different story about God, human beings and the world from the story arising out of the impact of Jesus and of the story about him in relation to the God known to him as Father. It is therefore to have a different understanding of the possibilities both of God and of man' (*The Contradiction of Christianity*, p.151). Now it is not always the case that non-incarnational theologies are concerned to keep apart the divine and the historical, and many incarnational theologies are, we suggested, insensitive to the problems of history. But with these caveats, I myself prefer a version of an incarnational position. This might not have been the way things were and are, but this is how they appear to have been and to be.

3

I want to look now at the work of Christ in relation to the state of humanity past, present and future. It is sometimes said and presumably previously thought that a soteriology linked to an incarnational theology of the person of Christ guarantees a concrete identification of God through Christ with the political and economic problems of our contemporary worlds in a way which contrasts sharply with non-incarnational, generally idealist soteriologies. But the links between intellectual discovery, truth and practical life are not always direct. There appears for example to be little comparison between Frege's contributions to philosophical logic and to political theory, and medical research which has revolutionized health throughout the world has been done by the oddest individuals. The often indirect nature of the correspondence between theological propositions and socio-political recommendations is easily overlooked.

To say this is not, of course, to minimise the continuing truth in Bonhoeffer's aphorism from the German of the thirties that only he who speaks up for the Jews has a right to sing hymns in church.

The work of Christ, I have suggested, is a work of love. It is a work of God from beginning to end. The very considerable difficulties which attend our attempts to formulate theories about the nature of God's action in relation to the world need not lead us into too rapid transition from epistemological perplexity to ontological scepticism. The implications of the understanding of the work of Christ as the work of God include the consideration that all the analogies employed are transformed and qualified by reference to their ultimate source in the divine love: this factor is sometimes overlooked in perfunctory dismissals of traditional theories of atonement.

It is not necessary to decry man in order to praise God, to destroy man's understanding of his own dignity in order to point to new creation. In the light of God's love we can see the limitations of our own love, and appreciate the change which the coming of Jesus has produced. What seems to me to matter in considering accounts of this transformation is not so much intention, language and method as success in expressing the supreme decisive nature of the work of God in Christ. Where we understate the absolute centrality and decisiveness of Christ, then we have yet to attend to the full significance here of the action of God, both for the life of God himself and for humanity. Something has already been said of the work of God here in speaking of the concept of God and the person of Christ, and we shall return to this aspect.

The work of Christ is also *par excellence* a work of man of the man Jesus of Nazareth. In focusing upon man we need not, as is sometimes feared, abandon talk of God. 'For Jesus himself God was surely something immeasurably more than a functionally valid idea. He was the central reality of his experience, the recipient of his love and obedience, the sustaining ground of his action and the source and goal of his hope'.[5] It is as intelligible to speak of the work of God as it is to speak of the work of man, but in the latter case our rational grounds for such talk are more susceptible of elements at least of empirical and historical verification. Though even here caution is necessary, for our theories about Jesus' activities, personality and social and political attitudes appear to be considerably underdetermined by the available facts.

Salvation through Christ depends upon Jesus' humanity. How can one combine such a humanity with the element of 'more than human' indicated in my account of God's involvement in incarnation without docetism, or the old 'paradox' dilemma? In part, perhaps, by avoiding the suggestion of a parallelism and direct correspondence between divine and human attributes in Christ. I would look for the sinlessness of Jesus, for example, not so much in a unique ontological difference from us *qua* human being as in the will to avoid certain sorts of action which would compromise the divine love because they did not reflect God's character of self-giving.

Here the lasting value of exemplarist theories of atonement can be appreciated. Theories of atonement must evidently include both 'subjective' and 'objective' elements. Simply because men may not always be in a position to respond to a moral example does not take away its intrinsic worth as a deed done. The protest of a nameless sufferer in an anonymous labour camp is no less valid than the gesture of a celebrity in the lights of the media. We have little detailed information about Jesus' mental and physical struggles from the paltry historical evidence available.

Perhaps we should not distrust too much our powers of imagination to conceive the sort of challenge that must have been faced and overcome. To underestimate the human cost of our salvation is to underestimate the depth of its significance.

4

Still, it may be said, we have yet to specify wherein salvation lies. Are we in fact justified or sanctified or both, is our justification real or imputed, are we rescued from the devil, granted forgiveness from our sin of total depravity by the satisfaction made by Christ in penal substitution in our place before God's wrath? Are we gently encouraged along the path of inevitable human progress, are we saved for fulfilment in this life, or the next, and what sort of fulfilment is offered, deification, humanization, socialization or whatever?

We can scarcely consider the mystery of man's salvation without some reflection upon the mystery of man.[6] In theology we are concerned with a doctrine of man which should be neither insulated from nor parasitic upon knowledge derived from other disciplines. Our concern is man before God, but man in intimate connection with all his fellow men. As such we are bound to have problems with any simple model. How can we produce an identikit picture of all the men and women who live, who have lived, who will live? We must presumably maintain some understanding of the inbuilt tension between the goodness of God's creation and the reality of contradiction, disaster and evil. We are created to love God and our fellow man, but for various reasons our relationships, though continuing, become strained. Relations are restored, at least in anticipation, by God. We know something of love wherever in the world there is goodness done. In the life of Jesus we see the divine love in all its depth as the disclosure of the nature of God. Nature and grace are not irreconcilable opposites, but everything hangs on the way in which they are understood to be brought together. Salvation is from God, to God, but includes the humanization of mankind. It has significant eschatological dimensions, but it is concerned too with the life of the human community here and now.

This brings me, in brief parenthesis, to the relations between salvation through Christ to salvation in other religions and non-theological understandings of fulfilment. The Christian faith appears to me to be dialectically related to the phenomenon of religion. It is not, as has been sometimes thought, the abolition of religion, but it judges religion as it judges all else, including itself. This sort of distinction is sometimes made in an effort to upstage all other religions on behalf of the claims of Christianity. But it could also apply to other religions in a similar way. All major religions are engaged with all aspects of the phenomenon of the human and for Christian theology to engage in discussion with non-theological anthropological concerns is not to exclude, precisely at the same time, conversation with other religions.[7]

But it may be thought that I have defined salvation through Christ in such a way as to discount the claims of other ways of salvation. I hope that I have not. I may hope perhaps to contribute to talk of human fulfilment in a human community of which large sections believe belief in God to be groundless by speaking of a quality of corporate life and corporate concern which, though it derives from God's love, may be hoped to be capable of commending itself in the long term on the basis of its own human credentials, because it reflects the truth of what God has created us to be, and keeps open for us, as part of the divine condition of human freedom.[8] And since God is truth, I trust that he becomes known in his own way in his own time. The position with other religions may not be too dissimilar.

Here then is a bond of belief in transcendent values, both

in theistic and non-theistic religions. Like all things finite, these beliefs can be helpful in understanding God. But when I speak of a quality of corporate concern deriving from God's love, I believe that this love will be seen, perhaps first in an eschatological dimension, to be grounded in the life, death and resurrection of Christ. This is a difficult area, for it is clear that wherever we seek to defend the Gospel by positivist propaganda we betray it. I have still contrived to say nothing about a host of problems concerning salvation through Christ, but I must now attempt to draw some of these reflections together.

Salvation as I understand it is in its most comprehensive sense the final goal to which God wills to bring his creatures in relationship with himself in the eschatological future. As such it remains to some extent unknown to us between the times, and all our images of it are provisional. It is not entirely unknown, for it will correspond to the nature of God who is infinite love. We may hope to justify this talk of the future on the basis of grounds in the present. If we cannot do so, it is less than reasonable to proceed further. We believe that the future is to some extent anticipated in the present because of the events concerning Jesus in the past and the life of the Christian community. These events provide the clues, at once reliable and incomplete, to our understanding of salvation.

I want to interpret the story of Jesus against the background of the Judaeo-Christian understanding of the relation of creator to creation. Salvation includes a personal relationship for all human beings with God: anything less is inadequate to the testimony of those who have lived in this tradition. Such a relationship is obviously open to excessively anthropomorphic interpretation. But the abuse need not take away proper use, and I see no need to regard those who have spoken in this way as having been mistaken. It is likely that most people who have lived and died have been unaware of this relationship, but this does not make the existence of the bond less significant.

I lay stress then on the relationship of the divine love to all creation. But this love has been further worked out in God's involvement in the contingency of the created order in his engagement with a single human life through Jesus. Here is identification with neither reservation nor absorption in the human. As I understand it, this sort of proposal is neither a result of purely historical observation nor of logical deduction nor an attempt to make sense of the world in relation to God or man. It is more a reasoned conclusion from the complex state of affairs involving the activity of Jesus, the Judaeo-Christian tradition and Christian experience of God and of human life since New Testament times.

God is involved, I suggest, in a way which remains to us largely unknown, in Jesus' life. This experience included death, though God does not himself die, and the overcoming of human death. Jesus lives a completely human life in devotion to God and his fellows, spelling out in teaching and in action the nature of God's love. But he dies, at the hands of the civil and religious powers. Is the fact that he died in conflict, and not peacefully in bed at a great age, just another of the many details of the biblical narratives which we no longer want to press? It appears that the manner of his dying is central to an understanding of his theological significance. He died as a human example of human integrity and a witness to a particular understanding of God. In this way Jesus has taken our sins upon himself in a metaphorical but none the less powerful manner, exposing the contrast between the divine love and all shades of grey in lesser loves.

But when the creator becomes directly involved in creation more takes place. This is indicated by the events surrounding the resurrection. What exactly happened we shall never, in the nature of the case, be able to say. But this does not make the resurrection a meaningless event to be accepted as a miracle *sola fide*. The resurrection indicates the significance of the life and death which have preceded it. The new age has dawned. The divine love has in some fundamental sense triumphed in *concreto*, within the created order over evil. In that sense there has been cosmic victory, judgement upon the unloving, a new way opened for a renewed humanity.

We can see that the traditional imagery of salvation from chaos, satisfaction and even substitution, judgement in our place, was by no means unperceptive. There is a great gap between God's love and ours, between creator and creature. Only God's personal involvement in human life and death has bridged the gap, and this precisely through indentification with the human response of Jesus, has done what we could not do for ourselves.

What reasons do we have, however, to justify the use of the kerugmatic 'for us'?[9] We live no longer in a world of universal categories in which we can move easily across time and space from the one to the many. The justification must lie, I suppose, as far as we can produce justification, once again in the relationship between God the creator and Jesus and God the creator and us. It is because Jesus was involved with God that he is involved with us, and because God was involved with Jesus that he is involved with us in a way that takes up his experience through Jesus. God is no longer as he was, having made himself subject to change. But since this change was decisive, he is not about to change again. God's being is for ever bound up with the experience of historicality, but it is not permanently subject to the limitations of historicality (doctrine of the Spirit of the risen Christ). This word of contingency is important but not perhaps final. We should not perhaps allow the shame of flagrant Christian neglect of conditions in this world to lead us to forget the eschatological dimension. However difficult it may be for us to think of a continuity of personal existence after physical disintegration, such continuation is a central aspect of salvation through Christ, without which the whole would be even less comprehensible than it is: again the clue now is the evidence of the divine love in the story of Jesus and in Christian reflection upon it.

I have spoken of the gulf between the love of God and the

love of man. This is an invitation neither to pietism nor to disparagement of human progress. It is obviously all the more incumbent upon people who hope to have understood anything of God's love to appreciate and support any sort of compassionate concern for others, and to react to its absence in all individual and social contexts. Salvation through Christ remains, as I see it, from whatever theological perspective it is considered, God's permanent invitation to participation in his new creation, which includes the humanization of mankind.[10] This humanization is to be completed, perhaps not in the deification of man, but in the humanization of man in God for ever.[11]

Notes to Chapter 10

1 cf. R. S. Franks, *The Work of Christ* (Nelson, London, 1962).
2 cf. M. F. Wiles, *The Making of Christian Doctrine*, 94ff, and *Working Papers in Doctrine*, 108ff (SCM Press, London, 1976). cf. G. W. H. Lampe in *God as Spirit* (OUP, 1977).
3 cf. the discussion of the concentration camp situation, in *The Crucified God*, 273ff. But cf. Dostoevisky's atheist and the returning of the entrance ticket. cf. now S. R. Sutherland, *Atheism and the Rejection of God* (Blackwell, Oxford, 1977), and the discussion of evil in S. C. Brown (ed.), *Reason and Religion*, 1977.
4 cf. esp. O. Cullmann, *Salvation as History* (SCM Press, London), *Christ and Time* (SCM Press, London, 1952), and E. Brunner, *The Mediator* (Lutterworth Press, London, 1934).
5 Peter Baelz, *The Forgotten Dream* (Mowbrays, London, 1975), 86. On decisiveness and finality cf. D. Cupitt in *Theology*, Dec. 1975, and C. F. D. Moule, *The Origins of Christology* (SCM Press, London, 1977).
6 cf. above pp. 80ff on man.
7 On Christianity and other religions cf. O. C. Thomas, *Attitudes Towards Other Religions* (SCM Press, London, 1968), C. Davis, *Christ and the World Religions* (Hodder &

Stoughton, London, 1970), and E. J. Sharpe and J. Hinnels, *Man and His Salvation* (UP, Manchester, 1973).

8   cf. the problems of humanism, freedom and faith. It is point-less to line up 'the religious' versus the others. cf. still K. Barth on Christianity as the abolition of religion, on the ambiguity of 'the religious' as such.

9   cf. G. Lampe, *Christ For Us Today*, ed. N. Pittenger, 152. 'Grace is effective to create the reconciliation and to construct the bridge from man to God; and in Christ the human re-sponse of faith has itself been brought into being in full per-fection.' Such a position need not be 'mere subjectivism' as in sub-Barthian interpretation. cf. K. Barth in *Hören u. Handeln* (Kaiser, Munich, 1962), Festschrift für E. Wolf., 15-27, Extra nos- pro nobis- in nobis. cf. too D. M. Mac-Kinnon in *Prospect for Theology*, ed. H. H. Farmer. 'Subjec-tive and objective theories of atonement.'

10   cf. the WCC programmes on the Unity of the Church and the unity of mankind.

11   cf. too H. Rashdall in *The Idea of the Atonement*, 451 (Mac-millan, London, 1919). 'The sufferings of Christ reveal to us the love of Christ, and the love of Christ reveals the love of God.' On the relation between love and justice cf. D. M. MacKinnon, *Borderlands*, 90ff (Lutterworth, London, 1968).

*   Some of the material in this chapter was read to the SST con-ference at Bristol in 1976 and appeared in the *Epworth Review* for September 1977. I am grateful to the Revd John Stacey for allowing me to incorporate it here.

Chapter 11

God's Love in Christ, in Christian Thought

1

In speaking of the tradition of faith, hope and love we made reference to talk of Christ as the centre of the love of God in the past. Here I want to look at some further aspects of the history of Christology, with particular reference God's love. I cannot enter into a comprehensive or even representative survey of the history of the person and work of Christ. But much discussion of Christ, recent and less recent, inevitably relies on specific interpretation of the history of Christology. In presenting my own Christological programme it seems desirable to indicate the relation of my interpretation to others, and the consequences of these judgements for my evaluation of contemporary Christological proposals in the light of my focus upon the love of God.

Historical interpretation is inevitably selective. The consequences of selection can be illustrated by a glance at one of the best of contemporary Christological appraisals. In his *Christ in Christian Tradition*.[1] Aloys Grillmeier deals first with the birth of Christology, i.e. the development from the New Testament to the work of Origen. He then traces the development of the interpretation of the work of Christ along two lines which he calls the 'logos-sarx' Christology – through the Arian controversy into Apollinarianism, and the 'logos-anthropos' Christology through the Antiochene schools. There is much fresh material on the period especially between Origen and Nicaea, and especially on Marcellus of Ancyra. In a section entitled 'kerugma-theology-dogma' he maps out the further road from Ephesus to Chalcedon, through the conflict of Nestorius and Cyril. The Chalcedonian settlement emerges as the middle way, through the development of a modified version of the logos-anthropos model. The work is impressive, with constant reference to sources and a scrupulous attempt to be fair to all sides of the complex issues.

There are however numerous unresolved problems in the treatment. The logos-sarx/logos-anthropos scheme is a useful one, but by no means exhausts the possible ways of looking at the divergent traditions. The New Testament material offers too much harmonization and too little illustration of conflicts inherent in the issues. There is a one-sided emphasis on 'Jewish-Christian' theology, and imagery later to be discarded is not given enough weight. The entire period is seen too much from the perspective of the Chalcedonian telos, other positions being grouped equidistant from the centre to the right or left. The tradition, is given, known to be essentially correct, and needs only new language, perhaps a new 'hermeneutic' today. The tensions involved in rival concepts of ousia, and in different soteriologies as they sought to do justice to the historical particularity of God's involvement in Jesus' death are not fully brought out. Yet this is the work of a master of the subject. The patristic speculations of lesser craftsmen, often with the aim of establishing a prototype presence of a preferred modern interpretation as really or implicitly central in the Fathers may be passed over in silence.

The Chalcedonian definition of the faith is only central to Christian theology today if we choose to regard it as central. On the positive side, it expresses clearly a number of the central convictions of classical Christianity, notably involvement of God the creator in the salvation of mankind through his incarnation in Jesus Christ, truly God and truly man. Among available options it was as it were the best buy in the patristic supermarket, and retains an honoured position because of its long role in the tradition of the Church. But there are less positive aspects. It was a composite committee document representing a compromise between different parties and reflecting particular political circumstances. Though it did not intend to define exhaustively the mystery of faith, it was expressed in particular metaphysical categories belonging to a particular period, and these were intended, both at the time and in later interpretation, to have binding authority for Christians. It will not do to suggest that the definition was only intended as a form of logical grammar or a heuristic model; that would be anachronism. Though it may be held implicitly to contain the central elements of the Gospel, yet there is little explicit articulation of the human life of Jesus, beyond the formulaic 'truly man'. Most serious from our point of view, one might recite the formula daily without ever realizing that the God of Christians is in his essential nature, love.

One may of course read almost any document from an appropriate hermeneutic perspective in order to see it as embryonically or dialectically an intimation of one's own preferred position, but such a procedure proves far too much. Where nothing can be discarded, there is some danger of a surfeit of riches. As far as Chalcedon is concerned, one of the main difficulties in my view stems from its being a natural climax and turning point of the tradition of Logos theology.

2

The dominant category in expression of God's activity in Jesus in the early Church was of course that of Logos. The word was used in the ancient world in a very large number of different ways, sometimes in precise idioms and technical usages, sometimes in a general way, philosophically or non-philosophically, connoting a much wider or on occasion a much narrower field than is covered by our English 'word'.[2] Important for later theology was the development of the spermatikos logos by Zeno, the logos as the seed of all life, and the Stoic distinction between the logos prophorikos and the logos endiathetos: the logos in nature and the logos in the soul of man. There were developments of logos in Judaism, in Gnosticism and in the New Testament. Justin refers to Christ as the logos, but this is only one of a number of usages, which create ambiguity and leave the relation of God the creator, Christ and man unclear. Christ the logos is the arche and the dynamis of God, even the aionios nomos. Justin goes beyond Philo in understanding the logos as the only begotten son. But unlike the usage in the fourth Gospel, the logos is associated primarily with the intellect, producing illumination. The usage of the other apologists is more philosophical than in Justin, more influenced by Plato in Athenagoras, by the Stoa in Theophilus and with no historical or salvific significance in Tatian. In general we may agree with Harnack's comment that the usage in the apologists was practically unanimous, compared with subsequent developments.[3]

Clement took the model a stage further in working out a theory of the self-begetting of the logos in contrast to the Gnostic multiplicity of logoi. He relates the divine Son to the human Jesus through the logos, but has the unsatisfactory Stoic notion of the apatheia of the indwelling logos replacing the pathe of a human soul. It is only with Origen that we find the much more comprehensive treatment of logos and Christ which was to be the foundation of later discussion Arian and non-Arian alike of the classical fourth-century debates.

It will be clear from even this brief mention of a minute aspect of its development that the logos was inevitably secondary, in some sense inferior to God the origin of logos. Christian faith and worship seemed to involve the affirmation that God was in Christ in such a way that there was no

inequality between God and Christ. How was it to be possible to express this state of affairs, arising from life and worship, in an appropriate conceptual framework? How was it
to be possible too to express the salvific as much as the
revelatory action of Christ? In other words, the love of God
as a living and reconciling being needed a much more explicit and intellectually sophisticated articulation, if life and
thought were to be properly integrated.

All sorts of variations of logos Christology were tried. Paul
of Samosata appears to have concentrated on the will of God
as the locus of identity between God the creator and Jesus
Christ the logos: the man Jesus became united in will with
the divine logos. But will seemed to be less than essence: yet
where in a human being do you locate essence? How in any
case could you combine the essence of God, who did not
change, with the essence of a man, a man crucified, dead
and buried? Arius opted for the incarnation of the divine
logos, but not of God the creator, in Jesus, wishing quite
rightly to safeguard the sovereign transcendence of God. His
opponents of course concentrated on the indubitable flaw
that Jesus was then inevitably less than God. Nicaea in in-
sisting that the logos or Son was homoousios with the Father
pinpointed the problem, but offered no *explanation* of an
intellectually satisfying nature. Later Nicene thought explored the metaphysical development possibilities of homoousios, as referring to a state of affairs not simply to be
construed as a grammatical framework but as a parable of
metaphysical mystery. This was the best patristic solution,
but was infinitely susceptible to over-simplification in the
hands of the dogmatically naïve, and of development into
docetism concerning the human nature of Christ in the
hands of the more speculative, notably by Athanasius himself.[4]

The great and abiding attraction of the Nicene version of
the doctrine of the incarnation was its ability to foster a
devotionally satisfying soteriology. The unassumed is the
unredeemed, as Gregory of Nazianzus put it. If God did not

himself come right into human life, homoousios with Jesus and with us, then in Pauline terms we remain imprisoned in our sins: the incarnation did not work. But all is not in fact so straightforward. We noted the argument that Gregory's dictum loses force if the goal of human fulfilment is seen in terms not of deification but of humanization in and for God. God could do whatever he pleases, being perfect and lacking nothing, knowledge, experience or whatever by definition. If as a matter of contingent fact he has chosen to act in certain ways, this is due not to necessity but to his free decision. As far as the soteriological issue is concerned, an excellent case has been made for seeing concern for salvation through Christ as Arius' prime motive, and for developing an impressive Arian soteriology. To complicate matters further, both Arius and Athanasius were, we noticed, incarnational theologians, of different sorts. But it is possible, though we have not in fact opted for this approach for reasons given elsewhere, to produce a non-incarnational Christology of a sort that can speak powerfully of the love of God the creator through Christ in our world. The Christology affirmed at Chalcedon, representing a development of the Nicene formula with Antiochene modifications, cannot be regarded as a permanent solution. Its particular version of the doctrine of the two natures of Christ was to require further development, even within its own terms, and beyond this the future development was to be forced to find quite different frameworks, such as that of humiliation and exaltation. In all of this work the notion of the love of God in Christ is not forgotten, but equally it is not prominent. In part I include this section because I wish to relate the love of God as basis to the various interpretations of Christological tradition which colour so much of the contemporary understanding of what Christology is and ought to be about.[5]

So far I have spoken mainly of Eastern Christologies. In the West it may be said, in the broadest of generalizations, that the medieval Christologies, following Augustine, tended to be interested not so much in the nature and person of Christ, the shape of the fact of incarnation, as in the salvation brought by Christ to men. Anselm's *Cur Deus Homo*, perhaps best translated 'Why the God-Man?' centres on the satisfaction made by Christ for human sin.[6] This emphasis continued at the Reformation. Luther thought of God in the human situation, where can I find a gracious God?, rather than, what do we mean by the divine and human natures? (though he had his views on these too) and the answer came back to God as a glowing oven full of love. Calvin combined Luther with a new interest in the Fathers (at a time when new and scholarly printed editions were appearing) and seventeenth-century orthodoxy brought back to this synthesis the questions left over from medieval debate but still unanswered and residually still explosive.[7]

This is, of course, a nutshell presentation, though I hope not an inept one. Augustine was a student as much of the classics as of Christian culture, and his Latin Christology owes as much to Cicero's *humilitas* as to Tertullian's *satisfactio*.[8] The doctrine of Christ's presence in the Eucharist was a rich continuing source of Christological clarification, in Radbertus, Ratramnus, Gotteschalk, Berengar and on to Abelard and Bernard of Clairvaux. Above all the understanding of God's love in Christ was articulated in the work of St Thomas. There are two ways of the elevation of man to God, one way through grace in creation, *alio modo, per esse personale; qui quidem modus est singularis Christo*. The second person of the Trinity exists from all eternity, identical with God who is *ipsum esse*, being itself. In incarnation the son takes on a human nature in addition to his divine nature, already having a perfect personal existence. Jesus does not have a personal centre of consciousness, but this is not a defect. For what makes a man is not the person but the nature. For Thomas there is nothing new after the incarnation in the divine nature, but only in the human nature: the human nature is uniquely new in creation. So Thomas prefers to speak of assumption of human nature, rather than incarnation in human nature, which suggests change in

God. This is the best Christology in medieval thought. The difficulty, for a theology of the love of God, which Thomas *is* concerned with, is that God's self-giving for others in love refers primarily to the love of Christ's human nature rather than to the love of the creator in incarnation. This leaves the analogy of human love as the primary datum rather than seeing the human love as a paradigmatically authentic breakthrough of the love of the creator himself in incarnation.[9]

The effect of the great change brought by the Enlightenment as much as the Reformation was of course as decisive for Christology as for theology in general. The new Christology, from Herder to Troeltsch and beyond, looked for the divinity of Christ in the unique quality of the life of Jesus, as the man of compassion, and moral integrity, and inaugurator of the work of the Kingdom of God. It is often customary in contemporary British Christology to move from the New Testament and the Fathers straight to the twentieth century. This is not a particularly fruitful custom, for much that is discovered to be the essence of modernity is to be found, as we have already noted, in the pages of Reimarus and his successors.[10] As Karl Barth noted but others have been slow to discover, theology has still to come to terms with the legacy of Schleiermacher for modern theology.

'Christianity is a monotheistic faith, belonging to the teleological type of religion, and is essentially distinguished from other such faiths by the fact that in it everything is related to the redemption accomplished by Jesus of Nazareth.' Schleiermacher is the author of the Christocentric theology recently associated with the name of Barth but, as with much else, traceable back to the father of modern theology. The roots of this turn lie initially in the Moravian heritage, but more generally in the whiff of pragmatism and empiricism of a sort which characterizes the search for rational grounds for knowledge in so much modern thought, and with good reason.[11] The appearance of the Redeemer is complex and unique; it involves something new. There is a new focus on the power of God in human consciousness, and also the development of something originally given in creation, since the human race is taken to have been originally created in such a way as to have the power of bringing forth in due time such a perfect single human life. Awareness of consciousness of the power of Christ the Redeemer is grounded only in faith. Demonstrations of the presence of God, miracle, magic and the like can only hinder faith. This is of course a reflection not only of Luther's *sola fide* but of Kant's non-objectifiability of God, and the epistemological consequences which are often thought to follow from the metaphysical state of affairs. Though the perfect form (eidos) of God, Christ is a being completely involved in history, conditioned by his times and background. In his appearance God's creative act and the development of the human race come together. The saving element is not his death or his resurrection but his person. Like Barth and many others, Schleiermacher saw his own Christology as a development of the Christ of the Johannine prologue.

When we reflect on the implications of our concept of the love of God for a Christology like that of Schleiermacher, we notice that there is little explicit attempt to speak of the nature of the action of God in the work of Christ, and little concentration on the areas of crucifixion, and resurrection which were important for our account of the self-giving of the creator in salvation. At the same time, the joining together of many traditional categories produced a new understanding of redemption, and stress on the relation of the redemption in Christ to the community and to all mankind was entirely fruitful. Richard Niebuhr has well said that 'Schleiermacher's weakness is that he does not give to Christ, in his thinking about God, nearly the same power of reforming the mode of thought that he allows him in his thinking about man'.[12] On the other hand, recalling what we said apropos Barth and Schleiermacher in speaking of truth in theology, a suitably modified understanding of the divine self-awareness may open the way to wider consideration of God's being as in its essential nature personal love, in a developed understanding of personhood. Such considerations differ considerably from the more usual approaches to the development of the legacy of Barth in Christology.[13]

We cannot speak here of Hegel and Feuerbach, Nietzsche and Kierkegaard, all of whom have illuminating things to say about God's love in Christ. In Hegel's brilliantly comprehensive theology, Jesus Christ was central as the perfect symbol of unity between God and man, the reconciliation between finite and infinite spirit. His contribution to the problem of divine and human natures was perhaps the most original contribution since St Thomas, and is still instructive. For Hegel the incarnation of God, and the reconciliation of infinite and finite are worked out throughout the universe, as we shall see again in speaking of his pupil Strauss. The life of Jesus, though it illustrates the truth of the way things are, makes no decisive difference to the world.[14] But alteration of the world, as Hegel's other pupil Marx was soon to underline, was needed. It is the claim of this book that through the love of God decisive alteration has occurred.

Alteration of the world, admittedly in the first instance more moral on a personal and ethical rather than a social and political level, was not exclusive to Marx's understanding of life. 'Christianity is the monotheistic, completely spiritual and ethical religion which, based on the life of its author as Redeemer and as the Founder of the Kingdom of God, consists in the freedom of the children of God, involves the impulse to conduct from the motive of love, which aims at the moral organization of mankind, and ground blessedness on the relation of sonship to God, as well as on the Kingdom of God.' It is by reflection on the motive of love, and by experience of God's loving will, that we call Christ divine. Love is here not only the result but also the touchstone by which we recognize the divinity of Christ as the focus of the love of God.

There are few theologians so despised in this century as Albrecht Ritschl, apart perhaps from his pupil Adolf von Harnack, and yet few have been so eloquent in speaking of God's love, and so deeply influential. It is clear to me that Ritschl's influence on Barth was much greater than Barth or his disciples have ever believed. And yet the neglect of Ritschl, and of the motive of love with which he came to be associated, springs largely from the legacy of those whom he most deeply influenced. In Ritschl's view, for Jesus the Kingdom meant 'not the common exercise of worship, but the organization of humanity through action inspired by love'. Such a programme could be turned easily into feeble moralism, and nationalist community consciousness. Yet Ritschl's was explicitly an international vision. The corruption of this theology of love where it occurred, was probably due to his avoidance of metaphysics, in the face of bad examples of metaphysics, and his succumbing to an implicit metaphysics of an uncritical sort in his own work. This legacy of anti-metaphysical theology was taken up by Ritschl's detractors as much as by his admirers. But if we are to speak of God as love, we must redouble, not abandon, our struggle with concepts of God as being, God as pure act, and all the other metaphysical dilemmas.

With Ritschl we return to the modern period. Ritschl, Harnack and Troeltsch will not solve the problems of one hundred years later.[15] Their contribution to talk of God's love in Christ is important, and arguably quite as illuminating as the patristic heritage with which, paradoxically, we are wont to be more concerned. By the same token, it would be entirely anachronistic to abandon the progress made by Barth, Rahner and others in this century. The love of God in Christ is no less present in the contemporary world as in the legacy of the past.

A final illustration of the way in which past and present must be tackled afresh in every attempt to recreate Christology is afforded by Pannenberg's magnificent *Jesus, God and Man*. Here there is a keen awareness of and masterly handling of the pre-Enlightenment tradition in the service of a new Christological structure. Light is thrown upon the old issues by a penetrating challenge to Barth's Christology in the present, and a return, which is also a fresh development, to Hegel's contribution. Largely because of the engagement with tradition in a contemporary framework, this is easily the best recent Christology.

I venture in conclusion to suggest, however, that Pannenberg's solutions are at best highly problematic and at worst often wrong. Often the most instructive solutions are wrong, and this does not detract from their brilliance. Something has been said about the difficulties earlier. Here I mention only the lack of adequate stress on salvific values. It is not clear how Jesus in fact accomplished salvation, though it is shown how he provides illumination. The root of the problem is the apocalyptic framework which is at the same time the master stroke. Why should we accept the apocalyptic framework, the expectation of Jesus' coming again, as *the* basic category, any more than Barth's Word? This is especially crucial for a theology which claims to be in principle open to historical verification on the plane of ordinary rationality.[16] It is not clear that Jesus himself saw his work in relation to eschatology, apocalyptic, and the coming son of man. On the contrary, as in the Sermon on the Mount, he was concerned with the effect of his teaching and action in the present. Again, if Jesus' opponents could not know who God was till the end of time, or at least till after the resurrection, it is hard to see how they could be guilty of blasphemy in condemning him. It is not clear that the unique historical particularity of the self-giving of God's love can usefully be compared either to indeterminacy in physics, apart from purely surface analogies, or indeed dialectically related to the totality of history in development of Hegel, especially in a world in which such metaphysical totalities are puzzling rather than illuminating. On the other hand, the careful attention paid to the problem of Jesus' resurrection is important.

It emerges I hope that the theme of the love of God in Christ is central not only to contemporary Christology but to the evaluation of the entire Christological tradition and to the further understanding of its courses and motivations. The examples cited have shown the dangers, but also the indispensability of such a dimension. As von Weizacker has well put it 'He who does not know what scholarship knows can make no contribution towards it'. This is obviously a daunting, not to say impossible requirement, but perhaps a useful reminder of an impossible ideal which, like eschatological concepts, may have its fruit in the past, even when only partially fulfilled, as indeed in the 'ontological priority of the future' – provided that we regard this as a useful imaginative rather than a definitive criterion.

Notes to Chapter 11

1   A. Grillmeier, *Christ in Christian Tradition* (Mowbrays, London, 1975²). cf. J. Meyendorff, *Byzantine Theology* (Mowbrays, London 1974).

2   cf. C. Andresen, *Nomos u. Logos* (Berlin, 1955), and R. Holte in *Studia Theologica*, (12) 1958.

3   A. v. Harnack, *History of Dogma*, II, 169ff (Dover, N.Y., 1961). A fresh assessment of Harnack is much needed. cf. the excellent article by E. Bammel in *Modern Churchman*, 1974.

4   Nicaea & Chalcedon, cf. R. A. Norris in *Lux in Lumine*, Festschr. for N. Pittenger, 62ff (Seabury Press, N.Y., 1966). On the understanding of Substance, cf. C. G. Stead, *Divine Substance* (OUP, 1977).

5   cf. M. F. Wiles, in *Remaking of Christian Doctrine* (OUP, 1977), and *The Myth of God Incarnate*. On arian Soteriology cf. C. W. Mönnich, *Netherlands Theol. Rev.*, 1950. cf. too C. Schäublin, *Antiochenischer Exegese* (Cologne, 1974). Paschasius cf. Grabmann. I.200. cf. PL.120. 1387-1490.

6   cf. J. McIntyre, *St Anselm and His Critics* (Oliver and Boyd,

Edinburgh, 1954), and cf. De Sales on the love of God, M. D'Arcy, *The Mind and the Heart of Love*, also D. de Rougement, and Gilson, *Spirit of Medieval Philosophy*, 273ff.

7   Calvin. On the seventeenth century cf. W. Sparn, *Wiederkehr der Metaphysik* (Calwer, Munich, 1976).

8   On Augustine, cf. J. Barnaby, op. cit., and my *Hilary of Poitiers*, op. cit. (lit.) p.110f.

9   cf. Persson *Sacra Doctrina*, 191ff op. cit., and Rahner *TI* i.149ff.

10 For Luther's description of God as a glowing oven full of love cf. WA 36.425.13 (1532) ein glühender Backofen voller Liebe, WA 20.693 on 1 Jn.3.1. Gottes Liebe ist ein glühender Ofen und WA 36.425, God as a 'Feuerofen . . . solcher Liebe, die Himmel und Erde füllet'.

11 cf. Reimarus, *Fragments* (SCM Press, London, 1970), ed. C. G. Talbert, esp. pp. 76f The Real meaning of 'Son of God'.

12 cf. R. Niebuhr, op. cit. cf. too H. G. Link, *Geschichte Jesu u. Bild Christi* (Vandenhoek, Göttingen, 1976) and R. Slenczka, *Geschichte u. Personsein Jesu Christi* (Herder, Freiburg, 1970).

13 T. Rendtorff et al., *Die Realisierung der Freiheit* (Gütersloh, 1975).

14 On Hegel's Christology cf. Küng, *Menschwerdung*, Kasper, *Jesus the Christ* (Burns & Oates, London, 1976), Fackenheim, *The Religious Dimension in Hegel's Thought* (Indiana UP, 1967) and ch. in Charles Taylor, *Hegel*, 197ff, 380ff, also W. D. Marsch, *Gegenwart Christi* (Kaiser, Munich, 1965). In this tradition, there is stress on the love of God in Christ esp. in Thomasius, *Christi Person u. Werk*, cf. too Feuerbach, *Essence of Christianity*, 52f.

15 Ritschl, Harnack, etc. Ritschl, cf. *Justification* 13. cf. R. Shäfer, Ritschl, P. Hefner, *A. Ritschl* and E. Haenchen in '*Gott u. Mensch*' (Mohr, Tübingen, 1965). His stress on God's love was taken up in the *Kenosis* tradition in Britain, by Mackintosh, Forsyth, Gore and Westonlite.

16 cf. Troeltsch's complaint against Harnack.

Chapter 12

Love and the Understanding of Christ

1

The function of Christological theories is at least twofold. They must first satisfy the requirement that they make accurate judgements about the nature and priority of the structuring elements in traditional sources which they seek, usually with new material, to develop in a new framework. The second function which concerns us particularly in this chapter, is to take detailed account of the problems for traditional theological frameworks which have arisen since the Enlightenment. This is not to ask for apologetics in the sense of a shallow accommodation to changing fashions. It is to give an account of Christology as concerned for truth within the concern for truth in the growth of human knowledge and understanding. Without such an account, which seeks to do justice both to the claims of Christ and to the real issues raised for the truth of these claims in the development of human knowledge, it is hard to see how progress in Christology as explanation of the grounds of Christian faith for intelligent human beings can be achieved.

The pursuit of a 'liberal' Christology over the last hundred and fifty years or so has had positive and negative results. There has been a valuable sifting out of the central and the peripheral concerns of Christology. There have also been vapid reinterpretations with neither the theological nor the intellectual strength of traditional affirmations. Most of the specific modern proposals are open, as their authors are usually well aware, to quite as many objections as the theories which they seek to replace. But at the very least, they may help us to lay bare the issues with which an effective contemporary Christological statement must engage.[1]

It will be obvious that I am convinced that theology has still to overcome the problems raised for its traditional formulations by the Enlightenment, and also that concentration on the implications of the love of God leads me still, with all caveats, to prefer a version of an incarnational Christology. In developing the Christological discussion I shall bear in mind what has been said about God the creator, his being and his action in relation to the world. Christology which is divorced from the doctrine of God the creator tends to claim either too little or too much.

2

One of the most recent and trenchant attacks on traditional Christology, which is also an attempt to meet the problems with which we have been concerned, is to be found in *The Myth of God Incarnate*, the subject, as one would expect, of much controversy, not all of it well-informed.[2] I want to look first at the piece in this volume by John Hick. In this clearly argued essay, relating Christology to the world religions, Jesus is seen as basically 'a man intensely and overwhelmingly conscious of the reality of God'. Incarnational language was appropriate to Jesus in ancient cultures. But we must understand its statements as metaphorical, not factual. Orthodoxy insisted on the two natures of Christ, but has never been able to give this model any factual content. To say that Jesus is God and man is little better than to say that a circle is a square, and the exclusive claim excluded most of humanity from salvation. If you believe in the reality of God, then you ought to be able to outgrow not simply

biblical fundamentalism but also theological fundamentalism.

Such themes are often criticized with vehemence in direct
proportion to intellectual insensitivity of the critics. Satisfaction with what Moltmann has described as a 'Glasperlen-
spielorthodoxie' may be quite as much a substitute for as an
invitation to serious theological work. There are often
unobserved difficulties in traditional accounts, and these
challenge the reader to think further for himself.

Christological statements are not simply factual. It may
be that the borders between fact and metaphor are much
less tidy than Hick appears to suggest, but it is clear that we
are not concerned with a plain choice between the literal
and the mythical. Myth may point to a spiritual reality
which is however dependent on certain historical data. He
notes that experience, as we suggested in an earlier chapter,
is never monolithic. Experience of Jesus' significance may
differ radically in different cultures. This does not mean
that it is entirely culturally dependent. In part it depends on
what it is experience of. It is hard to generalize on experiences so diverse as loneliness, watching the changing of
the guard at Buckingham Palace, and walking into a
moving bus.

The relativity of experience raises the difficult new question, new as a central issue in modern theology, of the relation between cultural relativism of various sorts of cultural
relativity. Relativism involves the whole of Christian God-
talk, as we mentioned earlier, and is not simply peculiar to
Christology. It is related to a second large question about
the relationship between criteria of truth and criteria of
meaning.

John Hick looks at the 'two nature' Christology, decides
that it has no literal meaning and classifies it as myth. I sympathize strongly, but I suspect that a number of complex
issues have to be telescoped to provide the solution. Much
language, and above all language referring to what we have
seen to be such a complex state of affairs as the ground of

Christology, has many strata, condensed only at the cost of radically altering the area of reference of which the language is used. The philosophical argument is here re-inforced by a reconstruction of New Testament Christology in which eventually poetry hardened into prose and 'escalated from a metaphorical Son of God to a metaphysical 'God the Son'. We must choose metaphor rather than metaphysics. By a happy accident it turns out that the original New Testament understanding of Jesus, and Jesus' own understanding of himself, are most closely related to the Christology which Hick prefers for the present day, and which is regarded as most acceptable, both philosophi-cally and with regard to dialogue among the world religions.

There is emphasis, quite rightly, that salvation should be open to all. 'If Jesus was literally God incarnate . . . then the only doorway to eternal life is Christian faith. It would follow from this that the large majority of the human race so far have not been saved.' Here we have been saved from biblical and theological fundamentalism, but may be in some danger of slipping into logical fundamentalism. 'The concern is not to minimize but to redefine Jesus' importance for Christians. He is our sufficient model of true humanity in a perfect relationship to God. And he is so far above us in the "direction" of God that he stands between us and the Ultimate as a mediator of salvation.' It is not entirely clear to me how 'God' is to be construed here. Sometimes the sugges-tion appears to be that in taking due account of other religions, we should develop a concept of God by conflation of numerous concepts of deity. This could become so general as to be hard to identify. If the aim is comprehen-siveness, then I suppose we should add concepts of ultimacy held by the millions who do not believe in a transcendent God (one thinks of China) and concepts of inner-worldly transcendence.

3

There can be no doubt that a 'theology of the religions' ought to be an important part of the theological agenda. Obviously too we can no longer use the language and concepts of pre-critical philosophy in our theology without further explanation. Stress too on the divine agape and its inhistorization in the life and death of Jesus is very much in line with our main thesis. The New Testament, brings us not a simple 'story' but an intricate story which in one sense can only be called a story by editorial selection of facts. It is, as it were, not a story but a library of salvation, including all sorts of different sorts of stories.[3]

We cannot rule out in principle a partly mysterious state of affairs in the events concerning Jesus. 'The event of Jesus' resurrection can be pointed to, but it cannot be fully explained in univocal language as most other historical events seem to be. That does not mean that it did not happen.' This does not of course prove that it did happen, but the possibility is not foreclosed.[4] But we may agree that those of us who speak of mystery should be prepared to explain as clearly as possible precisely wherein the mystery lies. It is this ability to raise problems clearly and forcefully, never retreating behind a smokescreen of piety and liturgy when the issues become difficult, which makes Hick's work valuable.

Analysis of the remainder of the *Myth of God* must lie beyond our present purpose. Something has been said of the understanding of transcendence in the work of Don Cupitt, and the issues raised by Maurice Wiles relate to Christology the questions which arose from Gordon Kaufman's understanding of God's action. Dennis Nineham questions the assumptions of some of his colleagues concerning the amount we can know of the historical Jesus. I sympathize with Nineham, though I suspect that his solution, appeal to ecclesiastical tradition, leaves unsolved the same problems that were left by Pannenberg's appeal to the tradition of universal history. We cannot do things for ever in certain ways just because that is the way in which they have always been done, especially when the reasons once adduced appear to us no longer to be compelling.

How then are we to produce an adequate Christological restatement? The more perceptive the discussions appear to be, the greater the difficulties that appear, both in the analyses and in the preferred solutions. The problem is posed starkly in Langdon Gilkey's fascinating study *Naming the Whirlwind*. Here the criteria of truth and meaning are collapsed into each other, or at least regarded as identical, in the manner disrecommended in our own discussion of truth. All traditional theological formulation then becomes meaningless, and the reference for God-language is no more than a synopsis of the plausibility criteria of the age. It seems that if we consider what 'the modern empirical man' is thought to find acceptable, the theology is in ruins. But if we ignore the real objections raised for theology by the history of post-Enlightenment thought, then our theology is intact but irrelevant to the real questions raised in the modern search for truth.[5]

As a pointer to God's unlimited commitment to historical contingency, not in creaturely existence as such but in the life, death and resurrection of the man Jesus, incarnational language, despite the manifold dangers, may be a powerful support to understanding the unlimited and self-involving nature of God's love. It is God's presence, then in Jesus and now in the hiddenness of the work of his grace, which remains the source of our understanding. But the imagination requires stimulation, and here the clash of concepts, incarnation and contradiction of incarnation, may be of value. Where our concepts lead to the impoverishment of vision, and so to loss of touch with reality, in relations with God or our fellow men, new directions become overdue. This can happen when we acquire an easy familiarity with God incarnate or with God anything but incarnate. The peace of God need not be thought to underwrite satisfaction with our theologies.

Everything depends on the nature of the case made for Christology, and on the details of the argument. Non-incarnational theologies may provide avenues of progress, and incarnational theologies may be comprehensive but valueless. I cannot myself think of a Christology which I would regard as adequate unless it included affirmation of a unique and distinctive self-giving of God the creator through a unique personal identification of God with the human life, death and resurrection of Jesus of Nazareth, a self-giving which is the focal point of the salvation of mankind. Whether or not such a Christology were to be described as incarnational, it would be possible for me to regard it as incarnational to that precise extent, and as adequate because it included the core affirmations indicated above. The crucial element remains not the designation but the nature of the specification, and its further value depends entirely on the details of the specification. Such a project has to take full account of the enormous diversity of the historical data. It has to combine faithfulness to the Gospel with recognition of the pervasive presence of myth and metaphor in history. It must exploit the truly radical implications of Continental scholarship for all God-talk, as much as for the Christological component, while retaining a sound Anglo-Saxon impatience with ungrounded speculation – not the easiest of tasks to fulfil.

4

Affirmation of God as the one who loves is certainly not groundless, but it involves an element of risk, of affirmation 'against the odds' in the face of an often bleak universe. It involves the possibility of being mistaken and is, like most theories in the natural sciences, 'underdetermined by the facts'.[6] But it is an affirmation which may be supported on many rational grounds. To come to the point relevant to

Christology, it is clear that Christologies which are basically a focusing or extension of the doctrine of creation require no incarnational interpretations. In so far as it is possible at all for us to entertain today the notion of a transcendent God, we can speak of a fully personal relationship existing between God and man, focused in Jesus as the centre of creation, without insuperable difficulty. But where Christology is seen within the context of God,[7] and God is understood as becoming involved in a uniquely contingent act of engagement in the history of our world, on the cumulative basis of reason, revelation and experience which has been built up in these chapters, then things become difficult.

I argued that the criteria for truth need not be identical with those for meaning. They do not become independent of rational grounds, but these are historical, metaphysical and existential. In reviewing the evidence for Christology it seems to me that this points to a unique involvement of God in our world, in which God is himself involved in a mysterious act of self-giving, self-abandonment and self-affirmation. The grounds for this judgement are partly traditional, partly modern. They are not conclusive, but not insignificant, and involve assessing the life, death and resurrection of Jesus in the New Testament and in Christian experience, in relation to the doctrine of God the creator. I regard this evidence as pointing to a spiritual reality, but find it necessary to maintain a large measure of epistemological scepticism, to affirm truth, but not an exhaustive knowledge of how we come to learn of it. In others words, the questions of the Enlightenment remain on the agenda, at least in part, but this need not at the same time deprive us of perception of the depths of God's salvation. In affirming an incarnational view of Christology, of a particular sort, I follow the continental tradition of Barth, Rahner and Pannenberg, without sharing their epistemological confidence. Such a position seems to me to be entirely rational, and to avoid the numerous sources of confusion which we have discussed. We said that incarnation as a concept has no particular virtues. We are concerned with realities, not indeed without concepts, but through concepts. Incarnation as a concept, repristinated from patristic discussion, is not necessarily helpful. But as a pointer to God's involvement in unlimited commitment to historical contingency, not in creaturely existence as such but in the life, death and resurrection of the man Jesus, it may become a powerful support to understanding the unlimited dimensions of God's love. The Christian Gospel is not about the relations of divine and human natures.[8] It is about the involvement of God in love in the life, death and resurrection of Jesus of Nazareth, for the salvation of all men. Salvation, we said, involved the life as much as the death and resurrection of Jesus. When incarnation is seen in its proper place, as a term secondary to salvation, salvation understood as God's characteristic gift rather than man's selfish preoccupation, then the understanding of God's love helps us to begin to understand the place of Christ in Christian faith. Given that all the terms used in Christological discussion have advantages and disadvantages, I want to set out now some account of the mystery of Christ, as I understand this, in the light of the love of God.

God in the Judaeo-Christian tradition is both creator and redeemer, infinetly transcendent to and intimately present to his creation, active in self-giving love, creating and sustaining relationships with his creatures. We have been attempting to build up a case for a rational reaffirmation of faith in this God in the modern world. Distinctively Christian faith is focused however on the relation to God and man of Jesus of Nazareth. Our concern is not only with the transcendent God but also with a man in history, within a web of historical contingency and cultural relativity,[9] Jesus lives and dies as a man of heroic integrity, teaching of the breaking in of God's kingdom through his own activity. He dies, and a community grows up which confesses that God has raised Jesus from death, inaugurating a new creation, in which new relationships between God and man, men and men, life and death are opened up.

Here God the creator of the universe is involved in a series of acts of self-giving which includes the element of self-abandonment in which God takes death overcome into his own experience as God. Here the creator sets the personal and intimate relation which he has already established with his creation on a new basis, still open as before to contingencies of finite human freedom, not discontinuous with his previous action but enriching the potential of the universe immeasurably. God's love operates by engendering more love.

This, as I understand it, is part of the truth of God's incarnation in Jesus. It is truth infinitely complex for our complete understanding, open to endless misinterpretation. This is God's mystery. It will not easily be understood by repeating traditional formulas nor by demolishing them. It is a truth which does not change, but since the intellectual communities in which we live change rapidly, it must be thought through afresh in every generation.

Incarnation must also be linked constantly with salvation, if the love of God in Christ is to be adequately understood. Neither focal concept need to played off against the other. We commented on the folly of dismissing non-incarnational theologies with the aid of off-the-peg incarnational slogans and vice-versa.

A fortiori, the same applies to exclusive concentration on incarnation rather than atonement, soteriology rather than Christology, the subjective rather than the objective, the cross rather than the life and the resurrection, *pro me* rather than *extra nos*, and other pairs of overlapping but by means identical juxtapositions. The love of God expresses itself in personal relationships which leads mankind and creation towards the goal to which God has always been directing, and persuading. Salvation is the natural, but immensely difficult and complex, fulfilment of creation.

Let me attempt to indicate precisely wherein the mystery lies. I spoke of God taking the experience of death into his own history, destroying death through the crucifixion and resurrection of Jesus. In speaking of the infinite transcendent God I am using metaphorical language. This language employs analogy, suggesting likeness and unlikeness. It rests partly on parable, God's parable and men's parables. It involves mythological and literal, scientific, literary, historical and numerous other strands. I am not, however, saying that God is metaphorically involved in death.[11] I am making an affirmation about the truth of a state of affairs involving ultimate spiritual reality, God, a truth which involves the physical reality of both Jesus' life and our own. This affirmation goes against much of the reality of human struggles for existence, is made 'against the odds', but would precisely for that reason be pointless if it were thought to be groundless.

How God may take death overcome into his own experience as God we shall never, it seems, be able to say. But that that is what we want still to affirm about God is a momentous conclusion. In the past Christians have sometimes believed that they could understand how this could take place. The collapse of these reasons led to the collapse of confidence in God. It seems to me to be crucially important to realize that we may still have faith in an informed understanding of the love of God in Christ without the traditional epistemological confidence. To begin to appreciate the great complexity of God's relations with us in his love may become an invitation, not to despair of God, but to come to love him more deeply, and so to reach a more profound understanding.

Here the Christological discussion leads us back to the nature of the Christian God, for whom to be is to love. I spoke of God's love in Christ as a spiritual reality. 'Spiritual reality' has deservedly a bad name in theology and philosophy, due to a thousand years of Platonizing neglect of this world as God's good creation, and this world's problems as real and frightening problems to be coped with within creation. But the Christian need not be afraid to agree with

Plato that ultimate reality may not necessarily be best understood by means of criteria for knowledge which involve measurement by sole reference to historical events and physical features of the world.[12] He believes that the creator is hidden from us in transcendence at the same time as being known in salvation through Christ. This conviction can of course lead to all sorts of unnecessary paradox and mystification, but need not on that account be neglected.

Because God is radically hidden in his presence, and yet affirmation of his presence in Christ rests partly on grounds involving historical events and states of affairs in the world, of empirical reality, we are invited, it seems to me, neither to unquestioning ontological and epistemological confidence, nor to scepticism and agnosticism. We may share, will inevitably share, in all the doubts, half beliefs and perplexities which are at once the clouding of vision and the source of genuine communication with people outside Christian faith. But we need not confuse ourselves into thinking that we have no rational grounds for affirmation of the reality of God's love through Jesus Christ.

There is one further area of Christology which we should consider. Medieval theology spent much time in discussing the question of whether God would have been incarnate if man had not sinned.[13] This is clearly a speculative question, but none the less interesting for that. I have attempted to speak of Christ from the love of God as a positive new dimension in creation, rather than simply as a remedy for a failure in man's world. But we said that God's love was poured out characteristically on the cross because the nature of the human situation involved God in conflict with evil in the created order. It has sometimes been argued that the classical doctrine of the incarnation was built up in the New Testament and in the Church in response to the classical doctrine of the Fall, the implication being that, now that we regarded the Fall as essentially mythological in character, not relating to particular historical events, we should likewise regard incarnation as a myth. That is to say

Christology rests on a particular sort of mistake, and we need not imagine that God the creator was involved in direct intervention within the world in a special way in the events concerning Jesus. The main difficulty with this theory, as has often been indicated, is that though the Fall may have been one of many sources of classical doctrines of incarnation, it is by no means the only source.[14] It is also relevant to note that, though we may well wish to regard the Fall as a myth, in the sense of being unrelated to actual events in the natural world, we can scarcely regard evil itself as being in the same category, unless we wish to espouse the Platonic tradition of meontic philosophy and evil as *privatio boni*, the difficulty of which we have already indicated. It seems entirely reasonable to hold that though the cross is indeed the consequence of human evil, and engages with the moral and physical evil of the universe, still the incarnation is itself an inner renewal of creation, an opening up of a new dimension of love, which may be regarded as a natural 'second stage' in God's bringing of creation to fulfilment. In a similar way we may regard the bringing in of God's eschatological kingdom as a third and final stage, not discontinuous with the previous stages but still signalling a new horizon.

In seeking to articulate an understanding of God's love which engages deliberately with modern objections to and questions concerning the doctrinal tradition, we should not wish to lose sight of the rich legacy of discussion of many of these issues, such as the 'necessity' of incarnation mentioned above, in the history of Christian talk of God and of Christ, in patristic, medieval, reformation and later study. Our intention in this study is simply to concentrate on the immediate contemporary agenda. One has only to look at the careful discussion of numerous aspects of the development of dogma, say, in the use of the phrase Son of God in the fragments of Reimarus, or the remarkably sharp discussion of the scandal of particularity in Strauss's Life of Jesus, to see how much modern theological exploration owes to its past.

One vivid recollection of this ongoing Christian critique,

will serve for many, from D. F. Strauss, on the incarnation.[15] 'If reality is ascribed to the idea of the unity of the divine and human natures, is this equivalent to the admission that this unity must actually once have been manifested, as it never had been, and never more will be, in one individual? This is indeed not the mode in which the Idea realizes itself: it is not to lavish all its fullness on one exemplar, and be niggardly towards all others. It rather loves to distribute its riches among a multiplicity of exemplars which reciprocally complete each other. Is not an incarnation of God from all eternity a truer one than an incarnation limited to a particular point of time? Humanity is the union of the two natures – God become man, the finite manifesting itself in the infinite, and the finite spirit remembering its infinitude.' In reply to such sharp, honest and far from unsympathetic criticism it is pointless to reply with reinterpretations of Nicene of Chalcedonian formulae, however technically orthodox. It seems to me that a new interpretation of the activity of God's love in the humiliation and exaltation of Christ, in the resurrection of the crucified Jesus may begin to provide new pointers in response to our critical questions. It may be said that God's love is implied as the real substance behind much classical Christian theology. But if we are not in practice to form an exclusive Church, despite all our protestations of openness, freedom and the like, then the articulation and implementation of the intellectual and social dimensions of God's love as love cannot be made too explicit.

Notes to Chapter 12

1 On 'liberal' theologies, cf. below, pp.187f.
2 J. Hick, ed., *The Myth of God Incarnate* (SCM Press, London, 1977). cf. *The Truth of God Incarnate* (Hodder &

Stoughton, London, 1977), ed. M. Green, B. Hebblethwaite: 'Incarnation, the Essence of Christianity and The Trinity', in *Theology*, Mar. and July, 1977. cf. H. McCabe in *New Black-friars*, Aug. 1977, 550ff and Wiles and McCabe, ibid. Dec. 1977.

3   On story and stories cf. D. Ritschl and H. Jones, *Story als Rohmaterial der theologie* (Kaiser, Munich, 1975). Theol. Existenz Heute, 192. D. Ford PhD thesis, Cambs. 1977.

4   T. Peters in CBQ 35. Oct. 1973. 475f. On current Christology cf. the long art. in RSR, July, 1976.

5   cf. my '*Incarnation, Myth and God*', in New Studies in Theology, 1.1 (Duckworth, 1980).

6   On theology and the philosophy of science, cf. above Ch. 5.

7   E. Te Selle, *Christ in Context* (Fortress Press, Philadelphia, 1975).

8   There may be a reductionism which is a justified protest against the encrustations of tradition.

9   Troeltsch is here the pioneer. cf. A. O. Dyson, *History in the Philosophy and Theology of E. Troeltsch*, D.Phil. (Oxon).

10   cf. ch. 10 above.

11   cf. D. M. MacKinnon, *The Problem of Metaphysics* (CUP, 1973), esp. p. 73ff, Parable, Ethics and Metaphysics. Also Dummett & Wiles, op. cit.

12   For a defence of some value in Platonism for theology cf. E. P. Meijering, *Orthodoxy and Platonism in Athanasius*, 183ff (Brill, Leiden, 1968).

13   cf. W. Pannenberg, *Die Prädestinationslehre bei J. Duns Scotus* (Vandenhoek, Göttingen, 1954).

14   cf. Wiles, Baelz, Hick, op. cit.

15   D. F. Strauss. *Life of Jesus* (SCM Press, London, 1972), critically examined, ed. P. C. Hodgson, pp.779-80. cf. U. Asendorf, *Gekreuzigt u. Auferstanden* (Hamburg, 1971). H. Küng, *Menschwerdung* (Hamburg, 1971), 556f, op. cit. '*In ihn die Menschlichkeit unseres Gottes offenbart, dass in ihn gerade als dem Worte Gottes die wahre Menschwerdung Gottes um der Menschwerdung des Menschen willen geschehen ist.*' On Hegel on the love of Christ in *The Spirit of Christianity* cf. *Walsh*, Metaphysics, 143-4. cf. Jüngel, *Death* (St Andrew Press, Edinburgh, 1975) and ZThK, April, 1968, Vom Tod des lebendigen Gottes. cf. P. Schoonenberg, *The Christ* (Sheed and Ward, London, 1976) and W. Kasper,

Jesus the Christ, op. cit. (cf. my review in SJT, May, 1978) and v. Balthasar, *Love Alone* (Sheed and Ward, London, 1968). Jüngel, *Death*, p.13. The belief that God became man did not first arise *after* Jesus' death but was based *on* the death of Jesus and was only later brought into connection with his birth. On God's self-abandonment cf. Moltmann, *Crucified God*, esp. 149ff, 207f. On the Christological axis of humiliation and exaltation, cf. B. Klappert, *Die Auferweckung der Gekreuzigten* (Neukirchen, 1971), and art. in VF, 1975/2).

Chapter 13

The Love of God the
Spirit in History

1

Theologies of the Spirit and theologies of History often seem to come from opposite poles of the theological universe. Theologies of the Spirit often indicate conservative position, traditional stances and 'high' ecclesiology. Theologies of History in turn appear to have divorced the tradition and married the spirit of the age. They are good on theological demolition, weak on construction. In the first category come Orthodox theologians like Lossky and Bulgakov, in the second the name of Ernst Troeltsch, and more recently of Van Harvey, come to mind. Both words are however prominent in a great deal of 'Third World' theology.

Christian hope is the hope of love. But if we see a society of love in God's future, then we should be dissatisfied with present society and intent on acting in love on the basis of the fulfilment which we know God to intend for his creation. Christians have always believed that God did not cease to be involved intimately in his creation at the resurrection of Jesus, but was involved as creator before and after, after Jesus in a creation which was already a new creation. It is as God who has been involved in life and death and contingency, God as Father, Son and Spirit, that he now sustains and preserves his creation. How are we to understand God's love as Spirit, both in relation to the lives of men in history and in understanding God himself?

A useful way in to the subject comes to hand in Geoffrey Lampe's Bampton Lectures, *God as Spirit*.[1]

After the rather pedestrian, black and white style of a fair deal of recent theology, the sheer subtlety of Lampe's book makes a welcome change. The starting point is the meaning of the phrases 'Jesus is alive today' and 'Jesus is Lord'. Reference to resurrection brings us to the central theme. The Spirit of God is to be understood not as referring to a divine hypostasis distinct from God the Father and God the Son or Word, but as indicating God himself as active towards and in his human creation. The same concern for the unity of God, operating in 'a single theandric activity', leads to the conviction that 'Incarnation must involve far more than a physical embodiment of one who is substantially and personally God. It has to express the idea of union between God and man at a personal level'. Incarnation involves inspiration and vice versa.

The case for a fresh assessment of the doctrine of the Christian God is built up. Terms like Word and Spirit are descriptions of human experience, not to be hypostatized into entities in themselves. We are dealing with an incarnation of God as Spirit in every man as a human Spirit.

In relating Spirit to Christology, we must 'avoid the idea that in Christ God has broken into that creative process in which he is always immanent and radically altered his own relationship to his human creation'. What is decisive for faith is not Jesus the historical Jesus but the Christ-Spirit. This leads to a critical reappraisal of traditional theology of the pre-existent and the post-existent Christ, seen as source and consequence respectively of the fascinating but ultimately misleading theme of Logos Christology. As 'the Son of God became identified with God the Son' theology seemed to require the concept of a divine mediator, the Christian concept of God then becomes inescapably tritheistic. 'A Spirit Christology enables us to avoid this kind of reductionsim.'

How then can we encounter today the active presence of

God the Spirit? Resurrection involves for us a taking up into Jesus' life of Sonship. Belief in future life rests not upon an Easter event but upon assurance of the creative presence of God the Spirit. As we come to the Eucharist, 'the reality which faith receives in this sacrament is the indwelling presence of God as Spirit'. We receive the Spirit for the most part through human relationships. As Christians we may share in God's creative action towards the bringing in of his Kingdom. This is a distinctive sort of action. 'The Spirit which inspires love that "seeks not its own" is the Spirit of Christ crucified, and the cross is its distinctive mark.' God as Spirit creates Christlikeness.

The final section traces the Patristic development of the orthodox doctrine of the Holy Spirit as the Third person of the Trinity, which the model of God as Spirit is designed to replace.

2

Though this approach to the understanding of God differs in important respects from mine, there are also significant affinities. Both emphasize that the concept of incarnation will in no sense automatically solve the problem of Christology, both speak of the love of God in and through personal relationships. There are two further areas of contact. These appear in some respects to be far apart, and yet they are intimately connected. The first is the role of talk of the Spirit in helping us better to understand the nature of the God who loves as a God in whom there is an internal loving relationship, the area traditionally called the doctrine of the Trinity, and the second is the role of God in history after the events of Jesus' life, death and resurrection, in which, as Lampe puts it, the Spirit creates Christlikeness, the area of God's involvement with men in human society.

Geoffrey Lampe thinks that the traditional doctrine of the

Trinity is inescapably tritheistic and ought to be dropped in favour of his preferred model of 'God as Spirit'. I agree with much of his argument, as outlined above. Many traditional doctrines of the Trinity are in fact tritheistic, just as many traditional Christologies are in fact dualistic. All Trinitarian models pose problems, but I suspect that there are also disadvantages with the God as Spirit model.

In understanding God as in his essential nature love, we cannot begin from any scholastic model, of the less sophisticated sort, in which God is a simple intellectual existence, as being conceived as a spiritual substance but in quasi-physical metaphors, or anything of that sort. We have seen too that, logos Christologies lead inevitably to subordination of God the creator to God the redeemer, and to inadequate appreciation of the relation between divine and human in Jesus. We have suggested a Christology of the resurrection of the crucified, closer to the Reformation models of humiliation and exaltation than to classical 'two nature' formulas. I would hold that it was precisely the danger of subordination, to which classical users of logos-derived Christologies were particularly sensitive, which contributed largely to the concern with complete, symmetrical equality and identity which characterized the Cappadocian doctrine of the Trinity. To this we may add the Neoplatonic framework in which theologians of the Trinity tended to start out from triads in God and the world of nature, and to look for Trinity as an arithmetic perfection. In speaking of God as Trinity it is much more desirable to begin with what has been termed the economic Trinity, and to look at the activity of God in relation to the world. Even where we may experience God as one, *opera trinitatis ad extra sunt indivisa*, we may be led by reflection upon the historical and metaphysical grounds of faith to see God as Trinitarian, in that he is engaged in humanity with the man Jesus yet remains God the creator, and operates in the world thereafter through the Spirit of the risen Christ which is a way of understanding God's activity in the world apart from, though not without, his sustaining creativity.

What appears to me to emerge from discussion of Trinity is that neither classical Trinitarianism nor a reduction to an undifferentiated unity will do. We need a more fluid understanding of God's loving nature in which there is as it were a constant shifting of magnitudes within the divine love, rather than some threefold mathematical symmetry. This language is inevitably highly metaphorical, but may be no less intelligible for that.

3

Christian talk of the triune God, as I understand this, begins not from the observation of triads in the ancient world, in philosophy and religion, in the New Testament or wherever, but from Christology.[2] God is involved in self-differentiation, self-affirmation which involves self-abandonment, in the life, death and resurrection of Jesus. The theologian understands God's engagement with humiliation and exaltation as the beginning of the death of death. After the inauguration of the new creation God's spirit, as the spirit of the crucified and risen Christ, is engaged in a new mode of participation in the created order. This new mode is what Paul Tillich aptly characterized as the new being, not negating the old being but adding to it a fresh dimension of God's personal participation in communion with mankind, bringing reconciliation not just to the faithful remnant of Israel in the Church but to the whole of mankind. It is in this context of cosmic renewal, rather than in the framework of an exclusive tradition of dogmatic orthodoxy, that we may best understand the role of Trinitarian exploration.

Trinitarian reflection begins then from Jesus as God's son, in the New Testament and in later thought. It is in the son that we have the father, and through the son that we have the Holy Spirit. The history of the doctrine illustrates the manifold opportunities which it affords for inadequate understanding – three persons in one substance like three bowls of porridge of identical consistency, and the like – as well as the careful precautions against misleading interpretation worked out in the tradition.

Opera trinitatis ad extra sunt indivisa. Opera trinitatis ad intra sunt divisa, servato discrimine et ordine personarum, and the like. The history of discussion of the relationship between the one and the three is littered with the names of the heretics, who provided nevertheless indispensable illumination of the problems – Sabellianism, Montanism, etc. All the expressions for oneness and threeness appeared to change their meaning with confusing rapidity. My concern here is more directly with the relationship between the persons. Concern to avoid subordinationism had haunted Patristic Christology, and led to a stress on the equality of the three persons so rigid as to rule out in practice any notion of assymmetry in the sense of different sorts of subsistent entity in the Trinity. Augustine's attempt to stress the specifically relational quality of the Spirit if anything led to greater caution among his successors, though his understanding of the circumincessio or emperichoresis, (slightly different ways of looking at the divine inter-relationship) as a relationship of mutual love was finely developed in the Augustinian tradition, notably by Richard of St Victor.

We experience God as one, as the tradition affirmed, and so, for Schleiermacher, nothing further of vital consequence was to be said of the Trinity – though in fact he thought it still had a useful role in characterizing God as intimately personal. But the tradition considered that even in relation to creation certain further distinctions in propositions about the activity of the Trinity could be articulated, as a further way of deepening of concepts of God. The doctrine of appropriations, as it was called, was not without value within the classical framework.

We cannot solve the problems of the present simply from

the past, and we must work from our own given situation. But provided that we recognize that our concepts are only a formal way of speaking of the complex and relationally centred God of Christian faith, then the Trinity may be as clear a guide to the talk of understanding as the notion of experience or any other guiding paradigm. Ian Ramsey in his *Religious Language* provided just such an intelligent restatement. My own approach would differ from his mainly in stressing the crucifixion and resurrection as the death of death, in an attempt to speak of the new eschatological dimension in a Trinitarian understanding of the Gospel, an eschatology not based simply on biblical messianic and apocalyptic sayings but on the love of God in reconciliation, renewing creation through the Spirit of Christ. I am happy to acknowledge that much of the tradition was unable to avoid the sort of disadvantageous hypostatisations which the prevailing cultures suggested. But at the same time, I regard reflection on God's love in Trinity, if not as the essence of the Gospel, at least as a still rich and underexplored area of Christian understanding of God.

4

I turn now to the second area of the Spirit's action. The Spirit of God creates Christlikeness. This is how we share in God's action in the world towards the bringing in of his Kingdom. 'The Spirit which inspires love that "seeks not its own" is the Spirit of Christ crucified, and the cross is its distinctive mark.' For Lampe this has involved constant engagement with particular political, social and ethical issues at a time when a sophisticated conservatism, favouring the status quo quietly, has often been the order of the day.

This is a stance which my understanding of God as love would endorse without qualification. At the same time, it is a conviction which may be shared by those who take a different view of the Trinity. Michael Ramsey comes very close in his *Holy Spirit* to the above in observing that 'It is a costly thing to invoke the Spirit, for the glory of Calvary was the cost of the Spirit's mission and is the cost of the Spirit's renewal.' It is in the shadow of the cross that in any age of history Christians pray 'Come, thou holy Paraclete'.

What is this community of the Spirit, how is it related to the Church, and what should be the role of the Church in the world today? It is tempting to write off the Church as an institution and to concentrate on the work of informal groups. Yet where there are already structures for the work of service of God and man in society, it makes some sociological and theological sense to work through them even when the structures require radical transformation.

Popular images of the Church are often scarcely flattering. The Church seems to reflect anything but God's love as the ultimate reality. Something of a weekend leisure activity, something of a complex of multinational bureaucracies, short of cash and even more of intellect, the Church appears often to be in pretty poor shape. In contrast to this Moltmann offers a firm perspective based solidly on biblical imagery.[3] The Church is the people of God and will give an account of itself at all times to the God who has called it into being, liberated it and gathered it. There is need for an inner renewal of the Church by the Spirit of Christ, the power of the coming Kingdom. Liberated from Godforsakenness on the cross, the Church may become the Church of the Kingdom of God. Its practice must include the element of doing more than others, but it cannot be judged simply by secular standards of success. The Church is the hidden servant of the Holy Spirit or else it is nothing. The distinctive marks of the Christian Church are as follows: 'Unity in freedom, Catholicity in partisan support for the weak, and apostolicity in suffering are the marks by which it is known in the world.'

There are gaps in this account. There is little attempt to

go beyond the biblical imagery, to argue out in painful detail the reasons for discrepancies between 'inside' and 'outside' views of the Church.

Sometimes in practice the Church seems to function more like a piece of semi-animated National Trust property, a piece of benevolent tradition within the structures of our restless society, delightful if not overdone. At other times a more unacceptable face is glimpsed, for example in the tedious power struggles endemic to ecclesiastical and theological establishments, often prosecuted most unscrupulously by those who are most conscious of their own moral and religious integrity. And sometimes, in places comfortable and uncomfortable, the Church does function precisely as the salt of the earth.

There appears here to be only one way of looking at things, a view not unfamiliar to readers of the later sections of Barth's Dogmatics. On the other hand, a Church which has no self-respect is scarcely likely to be respected by others, and we have here a constructive and imaginative account of how the Christian community may attempt to understand itself and its service to mankind. Whatever reservations we may have about charismatic movements, it is pretty clear that without some sort of understanding, however articulated, of the work of God the creator through mankind by the Spirit of Christ, Christianity in theory and in practice is doomed to triviality, however elegantly expressed.

5

Christian theology is by definition not ultimately an end in itself, but is intended to be the servant of the Christian community, and indeed of the whole human community.[4] It is not in isolation but through contact with others who believe, and in the context of worship and service, that faith comes to consciousness of itself and both understanding and commitment are deepened. The Spirit works through the community of reconciliation in Christ, the nucleus of a new humanity which is constitutively expressed in co-humanity. The community is not always faithful, but often divided, blind and unredeemed in its conduct. But it is still the life and witness of this Christian community which has transmitted and expressed the tradition of the Gospel, through the grace of God. This expression of love is not easy: Bonhoeffer wrote of the cost of discipleship, and Pascal said that Jesus would be in suffering till the end of the world.

The source of recognition of God's love as constitutive of a new humanity in the New Testament is the awareness of the forgiveness of sins and a turn to repentance, to a new beginning with God and men. As we begin to recognize the dimensions of God's love, we become aware of our own need for forgiveness and its fulfilment in God's reconciling love: part of the strangeness of God's love is its unreserved quality, indicating a horizon traditionally thought of in words like justification and sanctification. Luther brilliantly epitomized this dual relationship. 'A Christian lives in Christ through faith, and in his neighbour through love.'[5] But this love includes love to God, as well as faith and hope in God, as a response to God's love for us. The Christian hope too is the hope of love, and its reasonable grounds are the evidence of God's love in past and present, despite the odds.

The Church is indeed the people of God arising out of his relationship with Israel, saved through the new covenant of reconciliation in Christ and awaiting, as the pilgrim people of God, the fulfilment of his kingdom. There is a close connection between Christ and his Church, a dialectical relation of grace and discipleship, aptly characterized by Bultmann in commenting on the Johannine image of the vine as a trusting dependence on Christ as the source of life.[6] The Church is called out of the world: Bonhoeffer sharply and pertinently differentiated between the Christian understanding of 'worldy Christianity' and being simply worldly. The way of the cross is still a kind of dying to the world. But the Church is also called into the world to communicate the reality of the reconciliation of all men with God through Christ now. The Church waits for Christ, yet in waiting participates in the new creation, and so may become the medium of the love of Christ to all men now, if it is willing to be used in this way. As the servant of the community in the name of Christ it is eschatologically one, holy, Catholic and apostolic, but often falls short of its created purpose.

The Church waits for God in worship and service, but anticipates fulfilment in the presence of Christ through the sacraments. What are we to make of the notion of a sacrament in theology today? Luther said 'If I were to follow the usage of scripture, I should say that there is only one sacrament, and three sacramental signs'. Later he wrote, 'The sacred scriptures have only one sacrament, which is Christ the Lord himself'.[7] Baptism and eucharist gain their meaning from Christ who is the primary sacrament of mystery of God. In his life the secret of God's will for men is made known in history and is effective in history. His being is the *sacramentum fidei*. He calls for faith; to this corresponds the action of God and human response in baptism. He is a living presence in human life: in the eucharist a new awareness of this presence is realized and men may respond in thanksgiving. Baptism involves a coming to the community of the reconciliation that is already there. Eucharist includes memorial and anticipation, but also and uniquely, presence that is neither physical nor imaginary. Here we may find a fresh awareness of the presence of Christ in our lives, in the sharing of the bread and the wine in community, in the context of thanksgiving.

6

It is clear that the Churches, despite a great deal of effort, are often powerless to effect social and political changes.

Indeed it is always undesirable that they should attempt to take over the functions of governments. Whatever we may have decided about the marxist critique of Christianity as promoting a late-bourgeois individualistic ethic, it has been shown that the stand for conscience of single individuals or small groups, Christian or otherwise, is vital and not without effect in stemming the collective rewriting of history by a totalitarian regime, whether of the right or of the left. This is not a study in ethics. But we cannot leave the question of practical action on a purely theoretical note. I limit myself to two examples, the problems of poverty and racism.

Everyone knows that in Europe and America there are still many people who are extremely poor, and that the gap between the so-called 'Third World' and the rest grows greater every year. What is usually lacking is not the economic resources to reduce poverty, but the will to carry through the appropriate economic and social measures. Concern for the love of God can scarcely imply indifference to this continuing neglect, its causes and its effects.

Poverty is usually a relative description. Its bad effects on human life often spring as much from the comparative difference from the rest of society as from the lack of resources available. Those who have not, living among those who have, often lose self-respect, dignity and hope. This in turn gives rise to further problems, notably the apparent irresponsibility which often seems endemic in poverty stricken areas. Poverty effects the whole of a society, it becomes a way of being. As poverty leads to greater poverty, opportunities narrow and the whole becomes a vicious circle. Christians have sometimes believed that what was lacking was simply the will to work. The poor are lazy, and so sinful, and the compensations turned to, the occasional extravagance, simply confirms this view. Poverty is an endless trap.

It will not do simply to save souls and maintain them in squalor. A theology which neglects the specific consequences of the Gospel, whether it be thoroughly Platonist or scrupulously orthodox, is seriously deficient. If we ask why poverty still exists in societies in which there are the economic resources to eliminate it, then the Christian will see the root cause in the sin of humanity in general, alienation from God which leads men to build institutional systems to secure what they have acquired, and alienation from men, which excludes those who are economically the weaker. For exploration of these issues in depth theology must always be deeply indebted to Reinhold Niebuhr, especially in *The Nature and Destiny of Man*. The more it is questioned, the more tightly the defence mechanism for securing the resources of the successful will operate. Alienated from co-humanity man is alienated from himself, and the notion of service to his fellow men in time disappears.

If poverty is to be reduced, specific conditions must be created, through the creation of employment, training for work, improvement of living conditions, and of facilities for social life. But all depends not only on the will to plan but on the willingness to implement the programmes. The Christian believes that this is ultimately possible when alienation is overcome through the gracious love of God.

Similar tensions are involved in racism. Racism has of course long had the benefit of biblical foundation, the sons of Ham in Genesis being thought to have given rise to the Negro tribes of Africa and so being still under the curse of God. Modern science added the authority of pseudo-scientific certainty: genetic inequality is there in the blood, ineradicably. It is itself the product of neurosis, an expression of social disintegration designed to relieve a sense of guilt or establish self-respect, and damaging the racist as much as its victim. Racism is a form of idolatry, to which Christian theology is opposed without qualification, claiming that God in time in his love will recreate mankind, as part of the fulfilment of creation. An exactly similar response must apply to religious intolerance of the sort classically seen in Ireland. When we consider the sphere of Christian action in response to the God who loves, it is

crystal clear that we must be prepared to support the exploited and the oppressed without qualification. We must
act in love. But often of course the problem is not whether
we should love, but how to act in the most loving way. Here
all the resources of ethics, together with practical wisdom,
judgement, discernment and prayer, may be needed to tell
us to understand the implications of love in a given case. If
we are to support the oppressed in a political conflict then
the point may come when Christians must support revolution against oppressive regimes, and take suitable political
action. Much has been written of 'theology of revolution' in
recent years, and most of this has been extraordinary naïve.
Just as it was often believed in centuries past that God
manifests himself most intimately in wars, and this led to a
tragic glorification of war and a support of highly specific
theologies of war, so it is sometimes assumed today that God
manifests himself most clearly in revolution. Reflection on
the Love of God should help to banish any such delusion.
Theologies of revolution, even so-called critical theologies of
revolution, are no better than any other theologies.[8] God is
equally near to each generation, and equally abhors human
exploitation of other men, however lofty the cause in whose
name the exploitation is committed. It is sometimes assumed that Christianity has always been on the side of the
oppressors, the colonialists, the upper classes and the like.
Often it has been. Yet it is not clear that the decline of
Christian faith and practice in the modern world has led to
greater reverence for the rights of the individual, the
defenceless, the unfashionable, and the political inconsequential.

Our study ends on this note, of the central importance of
God's love, and the Christian practice and proclamation of
God's love, for the intellectual, political and social well-
being of modern society. Nothing is to be gained by avoiding
realistic assessment of and engagement with the problems
that prevent Christians from becoming fully the instruments
of God's love that they are created to be. Nevertheless,

above, beneath and through our collective shortcomings, individual and institutional, faith may still see God's love. It is in its own light, the light of the world, that God's love in creation and reconciliation is effective and will not be extinguished.

Notes to Chapter 13

1 G. W. H. Lampe, *God as Spirit* (OUP, 1977), Bampton Lectures for 1976. cf. my review in *Theology*, July 1978 and J. Coventry in *The Tablet*, 24 Jan. 1978.

2 On the early development of the Trinity cf. G. Kretschmar, *Studien zür Fruhchristliche Trinitätstheologie* (Mohr, Tübingen, 1956), M. Wiles, the Origins of the doctrine of the Trinity, *Working Papers* op. cit. 1ff and C. Stead in *Theology*, Oct. and Nov. 1974.

3 cf. J. Moltmann, *The Church in the Power of the Spirit* (SCM Press, London, 1977), L. Hodgson, *The Doctrine of the Trinity* (Nisbet, London, 1943). cf. Pannenberg, *Theology and the Kingdom of God* (Westminster Press, Philadelphia, 1971), 'The Trinitarian concept describes the particular unity of the living God, while philosophical monotheism is concerned for the dead and static unity of a supreme being as an existing entity undistinguishable within itself'. Though the alternatives are posed too starkly, the point is well made. Troeltsch. cf. too, The dogmatics of the Religionsgeschichtliche Schule, in AJT 17 (1913), 1-21.

4 cf. K. Barth, CD 4.3.1. and 2.

5 On co-humanity cf. R. G. Smith, *The Doctrine of God* (op. cit.), Barth, CD III 2, passim and Hoekendijk *The Church Inside Out* (SCM Press, London, 1967).

6 On Luther and freedom cf. Rupp, *The Righteousness of God* (Hodder & Stoughton, London, 1953).

7 On the sacraments, cf. D. M. Baillie, *Theology of the Sacraments* (Faber, London, 1957), Luther, Barth, Jüngel in *Ev. Theol.* 1966, 320ff.

8 *Theology of Revolution*, cf. Rendtorff and Tödt, op. cit., H. Peukert (ed.), *Diskussion zür Politischen Theologie* (Kaiser, Munich, 1969) and P. Matheson, *Profile of Love*, op. cit. cf. my *The Doctrine of the Church*, London, 1981.

Index

(excluding material in the notes)

Abelard, 45
action, God's, 104f
Adorno, T. W., 65
Althusius, 43
Anselm, 177
anthropology, theological, 127ff
apocalyptic, 126
Aristotle, 100, 132
Arius, 160, 175f
Athanasius, 176
atonement, 27f, 155f
Augustine, 37, 88, 121

Bacon, 113
Baelz P., 169
Baillie D. M., 29, 142
Baillie J., 100
Balthasar H. von, 153
Barr J., 106
Barth K., 16, 33f, 46f, 62f, 179, 192, 209
Baur F. C., 118
Bernard of Clairvaux, 37
Bible, in theology, 59f, 92
Biel, 37
Bonhoeffer D., 33, 162, 210
Brunner E., 54
Bultmann R., 38, 74

Calvin, 50, 77, 123
Campbell J. M., 27f, 89
Chalcedon, 172
Christology, 138f
Church, the, 208f
Cicero, 177

Clement of Alexandria, 174
cosmology, 135
creation, 94f
Crombie I. M., 64
cross of Christ, 45f
Cupitt D., 119f

Davidson D., 64
Descartes, 113
Dummett M., 64, 154

Ebeling, G., 38f
Enlightenment, the, 57, 98, 139
eschatology, 41f
evil, 56, 87
experience, 60, 90, 99

faith, 22f, 38f, 81f
Fall, the, 196
Farrer A. M., 105
Feuerbach L., 118
Flew A., 111
forgiveness, 167
Frege G., 64, 162
Frei H., 111
Fuchs E., 47

Gadamer H. G., 69
Galloway A. D., Introduction
God
    creator, 88, 95f, 135
    presence, 100f, 196
    personal, 96f
    hiddenness, 107
    reconciler, 138f

Gödel, 74f
Gilkey L., 190
Grillmeier A., 171f
Gunkel, 114

Habermas J., 68
Harnack A., 174
Harvey V. A., 126, 137
Hazo R., 45
Hegel, 104
Herder, 178
Herrmann W., 40
Hick J., 186f
history, 85f, 126f
hope, 41f
Hume D., 113

image of God, 130
incarnation, 160f, 190f
Irenaeus, 157

Jenkins D., 133, 161
Jesus of Nazareth, 19f, 141f
  death of, 147f
  resurrection of, 150f
Jüngel E., 103f
Justin Martyr, 174

Käsemann E., 40, 147
Kant I., 92, 114, 116f
Kaufman G., 105f, 123
Kierkegaard S., 58

Lampe G. W. H., 202f
Leibnitz, 113
Lessing, 115f
liberal theology, 185
Logos, 173f
Lombard P., 37
Luther, 38f, 58, 132, 211

Marcellus of Ancyra, 172
Marx K., 29, 212
Millar A., 64

Mitchell B., 64
Moltmann J., 33, 41f, 208f
motifs in theology, 14f
McIntyre J., Introduction
MacKinnon D. M., 170

Niebuhr Reinhold, 213
Niebuhr Richard R., 179
Nietzsche, 129
Nineham D., 189
Nygren, A., 34

Origen, 157
Overbeck F., 115
Outka G., 35, 54

Paley W., 99
Pannenberg W., 65f, 125f, 181
parable, 108, 119
Peters E., 199
Pittenger N., 48
Plato, 117, 196
pluralism, 91f
Prenter R., 48
poverty, 212

racism, 213
Radbertus, 177
Rad G. von, 125
Rahner K., 132, 192
Ramsey I. T., 207
Ramsey M., 208
Ratramnus, 177
relativity and relativism, 118f
Rendtorff T., 216
revolution, theology of, 214
Richard of St Victor, 206
Ritschl A., 48f, 181
Robinson J. A. T., 142
romanticism, 118
Rousselot P., 45

Sacraments, 211
salvation, 155f

Schleiermacher F., 62f, 114f, 178f
Schwarz, R., 50
science and theology, 65f
secularization, 122f
Semler J., 114
Smith R. G., 123f
Smith, Robertson, 114
Socinius, 140
Strauss, D. F., 115, 198
Spinoza, 116
Spirit, 201f
Strawson P., 97
Stoa, 76, 174

Tertullian, 177
Thomas, St Aquinas, 37, 58, 101f, 177f

Torrance T. F., 69, 72f
tradition, 37f
truth, 61f
transcendence, 54f
Trinity, the, 201f
Troeltsch E., 118, 178

Understanding, 53f

Wegscheider, 115
Weizacker C. F. von, 183
Wiles M., 189
Williams D. D., Introduction
Wittgenstein, 16
word of God, 31f, 80f
Wright G. von, 52